VEGETARIAN GOURMET

GOOD HOUSEKEEPING

VEGETARIAN GOURMET

SUSANNA TEE

Ebury Press
LONDON

Published by Ebury Press
Division of the National Magazine Company Ltd
Colquhoun House
27–37 Broadwick St
London W1V 1FR

First impression 1986

ISBN 0 85223 507 0

Edited by Veronica Sperling and Rosemary Hanson
Designed by Grahame Dudley
Photography by Jan Baldwin, Martin Brigdale, Laurie Evans, Melvin Grey, James Jackson, Paul Kemp, Peter Myers
Jacket photograph by Andrew Whittuck shows Ratatouille (page 127)
Computerset by MFK Typesetting Ltd, Hitchin, Herts.
Printed and bound in Italy by New Interlitho, S.p.a., Milan

CONTENTS

COOKERY NOTES

- Follow either metric or imperial measures for the recipes in this book as they are not interchangeable.
- All spoon measures are level.
- Sets of measuring spoons are available in both metric and imperial size to give accurate measurement of small quantities.
- Size 4 eggs should be used except when otherwise stated.

OVEN TEMPERATURE SCALES

°Celsius Scale	Electric Scale °F	Gas Oven Marks
110°C	225°F	¼
130	250	½
140	275	1
150	300	2
170	325	3
180	350	4
190	375	5
200	400	6
220	425	7
230	450	8
240	475	9

METRIC CONVERSION SCALE

LIQUID

Imperial	*Exact conversion*	*Recommended ml*
¼ pint	142 ml	150 ml
½ pint	284 ml	300 ml
1 pint	568 ml	600 ml
1½ pints	851 ml	900 ml
1¾ pints	992 ml	1 litre

For quantities of 1¾ pints and over, litres and fractions of a litre have been used.

SOLID

Imperial	*Exact conversion*	*Recommended g*
1 oz	28.35 g	25 g
2 oz	56.7 g	50 g
4 oz	113.4 g	100 g
8 oz	226.8 g	225 g
12 oz	340.2 g	350 g
14 oz	397.0 g	400 g
16 oz (1 lb)	453.6 g	450 g

1 kilogram (kg) equals 2.2 lb.

INTRODUCTION

Inspiration for vegetarian dishes comes from all over the world; in fact, some of the best cuisines – such as Chinese – rely largely on vegetarian ingredients. Vegetarian cookery is not a substitute for anything. Neither is it dull and monotonous. With plenty of vegetables and other ingredients to choose from, vegetarian eating can be even more satisfying than the meat-and-two-veg approach to cookery.

People become vegetarians for various reasons – such as humanitarian or religious, or simply because a meatless diet makes them feel better. Vegetarians who exclude meat, poultry and fish (as well as products of animal origin such as gelatine, aspic, lard and suet) are also known as lacto-vegetarian. Vegans, or strict vegetarians, also avoid eggs, all dairy products and – in some extreme cases – honey as well.

Many vegetarians also choose to eat a wholefood diet. Wholefoods are those in which nothing has been added and nothing taken away, so as much as possible of the foods' natural goodness is retained. In this book, wholefood ingredients have been chosen in preference to their processed equivalents and the recipes include dairy products.

A vegetarian diet based on fresh vegetables, pulses, grains, nuts, dairy produce and fruit, if well planned and varied, will ensure adequate fibre as well as the vitamins, minerals, carbohydrate, fat and protein essential to good health. However, there are one or two points to bear in mind about proteins. Proteins, which are needed for growth and repair, are made up of amino-acids. The body can make some amino acids itself but others, known as the essential amino-acids, must come from food. While the protein in animal foods contains roughly the necessary amount, protein from a vegetable source lacks, or is low in, one or more of the essential amino-acids. However, one vegetable protein can make up for the deficiency in another, so a combination of vegetables, pulses and grains will provide sufficient amino-acids.

Another point to remember is that pulses (this includes beans, peas and lentils), which are an important source of protein, are best eaten with a grain product. This can be wholemeal bread or pastry, brown rice, wholewheat pasta, bulgar wheat, buckwheat, oats or cornmeal – to mention but a few.

When cooking pulses they should (with the exception of lentils) be soaked overnight, before cooking. If, however, you don't remember or you don't have time, put the pulses in enough cold water to cover, bring to the boil, simmer for 2 minutes then leave to soak in the water for 2–3 hours until cold. Drain, then follow the recipe. *Always* rapidly boil red kidney beans for a full 10 minutes at the beginning of their cooking – to destroy the poisonous enzyme they contain.

Although lacto-vegetarians have no problem in eating enough protein, they still need to be careful to avoid a high intake of saturated fat, which can lead to an increased level of cholesterol in the blood. Eating too many dairy foods could lead to the diet containing as much saturated fat as a diet which includes meat. Low-fat protein is found in pulses, grain, low-fat yogurt and cheese, skimmed milk, potatoes and tofu (soya bean curd).

Variety is really the key word, adding spice and health to vegetarian cookery. Be adventurous, experiment with more unusual ingredients: with a little imagination and thought, hundreds of delicious and attractive meals can be created. You do not have to be a vegetarian to enjoy using these recipes. They give lots of fresh ideas for appetising dishes that can be enjoyed by everyone.

SOUPS

Soups range from light consommés to thick broths and from hot soups for winter days to chilled soups in summer. Nothing tastes as good as a home-made vegetable soup, especially when you have had time to make a good vegetable stock (see page 185). As an alternative use a vegetable stock cube but as they tend to be salty use less of the cube than recommended and add extra salt sparingly. The recipes here can be served as a starter or light lunch or supper dish. Accompany them with wholemeal bread, granary rolls, garlic bread, melba toast or croûtons.

ICED SORREL SOUP

Serves 4–6

100 g (4 oz) fresh sorrel
25 g (1 oz) butter or polyunsaturated margarine
1 medium onion, skinned and finely chopped
225 g (8 oz) potatoes, peeled and finely chopped
750 ml (1¼ pints) stock
salt and pepper
150 ml (¼ pint) soured cream
croûtons (see page 189) and single cream, to garnish

1 Wash the sorrel leaves thoroughly under cold running water and roughly shred the leaves. Then melt the butter or margarine in a saucepan and fry the onion for 5 minutes until soft.

2 Add the sorrel and cook gently for a further 2–3 minutes until soft. Add the potatoes, stock and salt and pepper to taste. Bring to the boil, then cover and simmer for 20 minutes.

3 Cool slightly then push through a sieve or purée in a blender or food processor. Stir in the soured cream and chill well. Serve garnished with croûtons and cream.

Iced Sorrel Soup

VEGETABLE SOUP

SERVES 4

350 g (12 oz) carrot, diced
225 g (8 oz) turnip, diced
2 medium onions, skinned and roughly chopped
225 g (8 oz) celery, sliced
5 ml (1 tsp) chopped fresh thyme or 2.5 ml (½ tsp) dried
5 ml (1 tsp) chopped fresh basil or 2.5 ml (½ tsp) dried
1 bay leaf
1 garlic clove, skinned and crushed
15 ml (1 tbsp) tomato purée
1.7 litres (3 pints) stock
salt and pepper
125 g (4 oz) macaroni, rigatoni or penne
4 slices of wholemeal bread
50 g (2 oz) Edam cheese, coarsely grated
basil sprigs, to garnish

1 Put the vegetables, thyme, basil, bay leaf and crushed garlic in a large saucepan. Stir over low heat for 2–3 minutes.

2 Stir in the tomato purée, stock and salt and pepper to taste. Bring to the boil, then lower the heat and simmer for 25–30 minutes.

3 Stir in the pasta. Cover and simmer for a further 12–15 minutes or until the pasta is tender. Taste and adjust the seasoning.

4 Toast the bread lightly on one side. Press a little cheese on to the untoasted side of the bread, dividing it equally between them. Grill until golden. Cut into small triangles.

5 Pour the soup into a warmed serving bowl. Serve immediately, garnished with the sprigs of basil and toasted cheese triangles.

Spinach Soup, Vegetable Soup

SPINACH SOUP

SERVES 4

450 g (1 lb) fresh spinach
900 ml (1½ pints) vegetable stock
15 ml (1 tbsp) lemon juice
salt and pepper
450 ml (¾ pint) buttermilk
a few drops of Tabasco sauce

1 Strip the spinach leaves from their stems and wash in several changes of water. Place the spinach, stock, lemon juice and salt and pepper to taste in a saucepan. Simmer for 10 minutes.

2 Work the spinach through a sieve, or strain off most of the liquid and reserve, then purée the spinach in a blender or food processor.

3 Reheat the spinach purée gently with the cooking liquid, 300 ml (½ pint) of the buttermilk and Tabasco sauce. Swirl in the remaining buttermilk.

CHILLED PEA AND MINT SOUP

SERVES 6

900 g (2 lb) fresh peas or 450 g (1 lb) frozen
50 g (2 oz) butter or polyunsaturated margarine
1 medium onion, skinned and roughly chopped
568 ml (1 pint) milk
600 ml (1 pint) vegetable stock
2 large mint sprigs, plus sprigs to garnish
pinch of raw cane sugar
salt and pepper
150 ml (¼ pint) single cream

1 Shell the fresh peas. Then melt the butter or margarine in a saucepan, add the onion, cover and cook gently for 15 minutes until soft but not brown.

2 Remove from the heat and stir in the milk, stock, fresh or frozen peas, the two mint sprigs, sugar and salt and pepper to taste. Bring to the boil, stirring.

3 Cover and simmer gently for about 30 minutes, until the peas are tender. Cool slightly, reserving 45 ml (3 tbsp) peas to garnish, and rub through a sieve or purée in a blender or food processor.

4 Pour into a large bowl. Adjust seasoning and leave to cool. Stir in the cream and chill for 2–3 hours before serving. To serve, garnish with the reserved boiled peas and sprigs of mint.

GAZPACHO

SERVES 4

1 medium green pepper
1 medium cucumber
450 g (1 lb) fully ripened tomatoes
1 small–medium onion, skinned
1 garlic clove, skinned
45 ml (3 tbsp) polyunsaturated oil
45 ml (3 tbsp) white wine vinegar
425 g (15 oz) can tomato juice
30 ml (2 tbsp) tomato purée
1.25 ml (¼ tsp) salt
green pepper, ice cubes and croûtons (see page 189), to serve

Gazpacho

1. Remove the core and seeds from the green pepper and chop roughly with the cucumber, tomatoes, onion and garlic.

2. Mix the ingredients together in a bowl. Place in a blender or food processor in small portions and blend to form a smooth purée. Chill for 2 hours.

3. To serve. Core and seed the green pepper; dice very finely. Pour purée into bowl and add a few ice cubes. Serve garnished with diced pepper and croûtons.

Spiced Dal Soup

SPICED DAL SOUP

SERVES 4–6

100 g (4 oz) chana dal
30 ml (2 tbsp) ghee or polyunsaturated oil
5 ml (1 tsp) cumin seeds
10 ml (2 tsp) coriander seeds
5 ml (1 tsp) fenugreek seeds
3 dried red chillies
15 ml (1 tbsp) shredded coconut
225 g (8 oz) tomatoes, skinned and roughly chopped
2.5 ml (½ tsp) turmeric
5 ml (1 tsp) treacle

1 Pick over the dal and remove any grit or discoloured pulses. Put into a sieve and wash in cold running water. Drain well and put in a saucepan. Cover with 600 ml (1 pint) water, bring to the boil, cover and simmer for 1 hour or until tender.

2 Put the cumin, coriander, fenugreek, chillies and coconut in a small electric mill or blender and grind finely. Heat the oil in a heavy-based frying pan, add the spice mixture and fry, stirring, for 30 seconds. Purée the dal in a blender and put in a pan. Stir in the remaining ingredients and 300 ml (½ pint) water.

3 Bring to the boil, then lower the heat, cover and simmer for about 20 minutes. Taste and adjust seasoning and turn into a warmed serving dish. Garnish with lemon slices and coriander sprigs.

CREAM OF PARSLEY SOUP

SERVES 8

225 g (8 oz) parsley
2 medium onions, skinned
125 g (4 oz) celery, washed and trimmed
50 g (2 oz) butter or polyunsaturated margarine
45 ml (3 tbsp) plain wholemeal flour
2 litres (3½ pints) vegetable stock
salt and pepper
150 ml (¼ pint) single cream
parsley sprigs, to garnish

1 Wash the parsley, drain and chop roughly. Slice the onions and celery.

2 Melt the butter or margarine in a large saucepan and add the parsley, onions and celery. Cover the pan and cook gently for about 10 minutes until the vegetables are soft. Shake the pan occasionally.

3 Stir in the flour until smooth, then mix in the stock. Add salt and pepper to taste and bring to the boil.

4 Cover the pan and simmer for 25–30 minutes. Cool a little, then purée in a blender or food processor. Leave to cool completely, then chill.

5 Reheat until bubbling, taste and adjust seasoning and swirl in the cream. Serve immediately, garnished with the parsley.

BEAN SOUP

Serves 6

225 g (8 oz) dried white haricot beans, soaked in cold water overnight
salt and pepper
30 ml (2 tbsp) olive oil
2 garlic cloves, skinned and chopped
45 ml (3 tbsp) chopped fresh parsley
extra olive oil, to garnish

1 Drain and rinse the beans, then tip into a large saucepan. Cover with 1.7 litres (3 pints) water and bring to the boil. Simmer, half covered, for 2–2½ hours.

2 Remove half the beans and purée in a blender or food processor with a little cooking liquid. Return to pan and add salt and pepper to taste.

3 Heat the 30 ml (2 tbsp) olive oil in a small pan, add garlic and fry gently until soft. Stir in parsley, then add to soup.

4 Pour the hot soup into a warmed soup tureen, drizzle over a little olive oil and serve.

ICED SWEET PEPPER SOUP

Serves 4

60 ml (4 tbsp) chopped fresh coriander
2 medium red peppers
1 medium onion, skinned
225 g (8 oz) ripe tomatoes
900 ml (1½ pints) vegetable stock
150 ml (¼ pint) milk
salt and pepper

1 First make coriander ice cubes. Put the chopped coriander into an ice-cube tray, top up with water and freeze.

2 Cut the stem end off the peppers, scoop out the seeds and slice the flesh. Slice the onion and tomatoes.

3 Put the peppers in a large saucepan with the onion, tomatoes and stock. Bring to the boil, then lower the heat, cover and simmer for about 15 minutes or until the vegetables are tender. Drain, reserving the liquid.

4 Sieve the vegetables, or purée them in a blender or food processor, then sieve the purée to remove the tomato seeds.

5 Combine the reserved liquid, vegetable purée and milk in a bowl with salt and pepper to taste. Cool for 30 minutes, then chill for at least 2 hours before serving. Serve with coriander ice cubes.

CRÈME DUBARRY

Serves 4

1 firm cauliflower
40 g (1½ oz) butter or polyunsaturated margarine
45 ml (3 tbsp) plain wholemeal flour
900 ml (1½ pints) vegetable stock
salt and pepper
150 ml (¼ pint) single cream
pinch of freshly grated nutmeg

1 Divide the cauliflower into small sprigs, discarding the green leaves. Wash thoroughly.

2 Melt the butter or margarine in a saucepan, add the flour and cook gently for 1–2 minutes. Remove from the heat and gradually blend in the stock. Bring to the boil, stirring constantly, then simmer for 3 minutes until thick and smooth.

3 Add the cauliflower to the pan, reserving about 12 well-shaped tiny sprigs. Add salt and pepper to taste, cover and simmer for about 30 minutes.

4 Meanwhile, cook the reserved cauliflower sprigs in boiling salted water for about 10 minutes, until tender but not broken. Drain thoroughly.

5 Sieve or purée the soup in a blender or food processor. Return to the rinsed-out pan, stir in the cream and nutmeg and reheat gently, without boiling. Taste and adjust seasoning. Serve hot, garnished with the cauliflower sprigs.

Iced Sweet Pepper Soup

CHILLED CUCUMBER SOUP

SERVES 4

1 medium cucumber, trimmed
300 ml (½ pint) natural yogurt
1 small garlic clove, skinned and crushed
30 ml (2 tbsp) wine vinegar
30 ml (2 tbsp) chopped fresh mint or snipped chives
salt and pepper
300 ml (½ pint) milk
mint sprigs, to garnish

1 Finely grate the unpeeled cucumber into a bowl. Stir in the yogurt, crushed garlic, vinegar and mint or chives. Add salt and pepper to taste and chill for 1 hour.

2 Just before serving, stir in the milk, then taste and adjust seasoning. Spoon into individual soup bowls and garnish with mint sprigs.

WATERCRESS SOUP

SERVES 4

2 bunches watercress
50 g (2 oz) butter or polyunsaturated margarine
1 medium onion, skinned and chopped
50 g (2 oz) plain wholemeal flour
750 ml (1¼ pints) vegetable stock
300 ml (½ pint) milk
salt and pepper

1 Wash and trim the watercress, leaving some of the stem, then chop roughly.

2 Melt the butter or margarine in a saucepan, add the watercress and onion and cook gently for 10 minutes until soft but not coloured.

3 Add the flour and cook gently, stirring, for 1–2 minutes. Remove from the heat and gradually blend in the stock and milk. Bring to the boil, stirring constantly, then simmer for 3 minutes. Add salt and pepper to taste.

4 Sieve or purée the soup in a blender or food processor. Return to the rinsed-out pan and reheat gently, without boiling. Taste and adjust seasoning, if necessary. Serve hot.

Chilled Cucumber Soup

CREAM OF JERUSALEM ARTICHOKE SOUP

SERVES 4

900 g (2 lb) Jerusalem artichokes
2 slices of lemon
25 g (1 oz) butter or polyunsaturated margarine
1 medium onion, skinned and chopped
450 ml (¾ pint) milk
25 ml (1½ tbsp) lemon juice
30 ml (2 tbsp) chopped fresh parsley
150 ml (¼ pint) single cream
salt and pepper
croûtons (see page 189), to garnish

1 Wash the artichokes well and put them in a large saucepan with the lemon slices. Cover with 900 ml (1½ pints) cold water. Bring to the boil and cook until tender, about 20 minutes.

2 Drain off the water, reserving 600 ml (1 pint). Leave the artichokes to cool.

3 Peel the artichokes with your fingers, then mash them roughly.

4 Melt the butter or margarine in a clean saucepan, add the onion and cook gently for 10 minutes until soft but not coloured. Stir in the reserved artichoke water, artichokes and milk. Bring the soup to the boil, stirring, then simmer for 2–3 minutes.

5 Sieve or purée the soup in a blender or food processor. Return to the rinsed-out pan and stir in the lemon juice, parsley, cream and salt and pepper to taste. Reheat gently, without boiling. Serve hot, garnished with croûtons.

Cream of Jerusalem Artichoke Soup

LETTUCE SOUP

SERVES 4

350 g (12 oz) lettuce leaves
100 g (4 oz) spring onions, trimmed
50 g (2 oz) butter or polyunsaturated margarine
15 ml (1 tbsp) plain wholemeal flour
600 ml (1 pint) vegetable stock
150 ml (¼ pint) milk
soured cream, to finish (optional)

1 Chop the lettuce leaves and spring onions roughly. Melt the butter or margarine in a deep saucepan, add the lettuce and spring onions and cook gently for about 10 minutes until very soft.

2 Stir in the flour. Cook, stirring, for 1 minute, then add the stock. Bring to the boil, cover and simmer for 45 minutes to 1 hour.

3 Work the soup to a purée in a blender or food processor, or rub through a sieve. Return to the rinsed-out pan and add the milk with salt and pepper to taste. Reheat to serving temperature. Finish with a swirl of soured cream, if liked.

VICHYSOISSE

SERVES 4

50 g (2 oz) butter or polyunsaturated margarine
4 leeks, trimmed, sliced and washed
1 medium onion, skinned and sliced
1 litre (1¾ pints) stock
2 potatoes, peeled and thinly sliced
salt and pepper
200 ml (7 fl oz) single cream
snipped chives, to garnish

1 Melt the butter or margarine in a heavy-based saucepan, add the leeks and onion and cook gently for about 10 minutes, until soft but not coloured. Add the stock and potatoes and bring to the boil.

2 Lower the heat, add salt and pepper to taste and cover the pan with a lid. Simmer for about 30 minutes until the vegetables are completely soft.

3 Sieve or purée the soup in a blender or food processor. Pour into a large serving bowl and stir in the cream. Taste and adjust seasoning. Chill for at least 4 hours. Sprinkle with chives to serve.

Vichysoisse

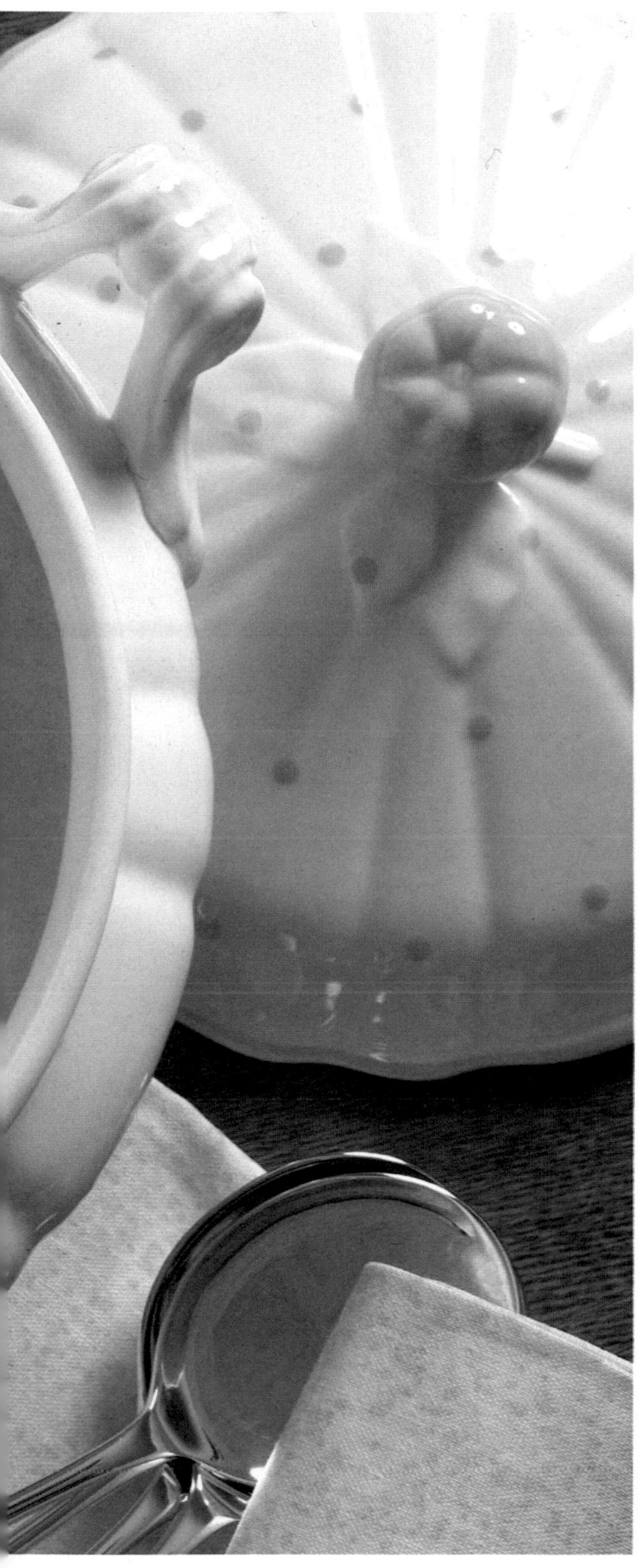

BRUSSELS SPROUTS SOUP

SERVES 4–6

225 g (8 oz) Brussels sprouts
225 g (8 oz) potatoes, peeled
25 g (1 oz) butter or polyunsaturated margarine
900 ml (1½ pints) stock
salt and pepper
150 ml (¼ pint) milk
30 ml (2 tbsp) double cream
chopped walnuts, to garnish

1 Remove and discard the outer leaves of the sprouts. Wash the sprouts well and then chop roughly. Slice the potatoes. Melt the butter or margarine in a saucepan, add the sprouts and cook gently for 2 minutes, stirring.

2 Add the potatoes, stock and salt and pepper to taste. Bring to the boil, cover and simmer for 25 minutes or until the potatoes are tender.

3 Sieve or purée the soup in a blender or food processor. Return to the rinsed-out pan, stir in the milk and heat thoroughly.

4 Add the cream and heat through, without boiling. Taste and adjust seasoning. Serve hot, garnished with chopped walnuts.

Brussels Sprouts Soup

CELERIAC AND STILTON SOUP

SERVES 8

50 g (2 oz) butter or polyunsaturated margarine
2 leeks, trimmed, washed and roughly chopped
juice of 1 lemon
2 heads celeriac, total weight about 900 g (2 lb)
1.7 litres (3 pints) vegetable stock
10 ml (2 tsp) chopped fresh sage or 5 ml (1 tsp) dried
salt and pepper
225 g (8 oz) Blue Stilton, rinded and roughly chopped
300 ml (½ pint) single cream
fresh sage leaves, to garnish

1 Melt the butter or margarine in a large saucepan, add the leeks and fry very gently for 10 minutes until softened.

2 Meanwhile, fill a bowl with cold water and add the lemon juice. Peel the celeriac thickly with a sharp knife. Cut into chunks, dropping them into the bowl of acidulated water.

3 Drain the celeriac, then add to the pan of leeks. Fry gently, for a further 10 minutes.

4 Add the stock and bring to the boil, stirring, then add the sage and salt and pepper to taste. Lower the heat, cover and simmer for about 20 minutes or until the celeriac is very soft.

5 Crumble the Stilton cheese into a blender or food processor. Add the soup and work to a smooth purée, in batches if necessary.

6 Return the soup to the rinsed-out pan and stir in the cream. Reheat, stirring, then taste and adjust seasoning. Pour into warmed bowls and garnish with sage leaves. Serve hot.

HUNGARIAN CHERRY SOUP

SERVES 4

450 g (1 lb) fresh red cherries, washed
15 ml (1 tbsp) raw cane sugar
150 ml (¼ pint) red wine
1 cinnamon stick
pared rind of ½ lemon
150 ml (¼ pint) natural yogurt or smetana (see box)

1 Stone the cherries, reserving all the stones and a few cherries for garnish. Put the remaining cherries into a stainless steel or enamel saucepan with 150 ml (¼ pint) water and the sugar, and simmer gently for 10 minutes until completely soft.

2 Wrap half the cherry stones loosely in a clean tea-towel and, using a heavy rolling pin, crack the stones to reveal the kernels.

3 Put the cracked stones into a clean saucepan with the reserved whole cherry stones, the wine, cinnamon stick and lemon rind. Bring to the boil and simmer for 5–10 minutes, then strain the liquid into the cherry mixture.

4 Sieve or purée the soup in a blender or food processor, then leave to cool for 30 minutes.

5 Stir the yogurt or smetana into the cherry pulp and chill in the refrigerator for at least 2 hours. Garnish with the reserved cherries before serving.

NOTE

Smetana is a cultured milk product similar to yogurt, but with a thick creamy texture like soured cream. It can be used in cooking exactly like soured cream, and is well worth looking for in Continental and Jewish delicatessens because it is about half the price – and half the calories.

Hungarian Cherry Soup

CHILLED ASPARAGUS SOUP

Serves 6

700 g (1½ lb) stalks of asparagus
salt and pepper
50 g (2 oz) butter
2 medium onions, skinned and thinly sliced
1.4 litres (2½ pints) stock
30 ml (2 tbsp) chopped fresh parsley
150 ml (¼ pint) single cream
small brown uncut loaf
butter, for spreading
thin lemon slices, to garnish

1 Rinse the asparagus. Cut off the heads and simmer very gently in salted water until just tender. Drain carefully and cool; cover and refrigerate until required to make asparagus rolls.

2 Scrape the asparagus stalks with a potato peeler or knife to remove any scales; cut off the woody ends. Thinly slice the asparagus stalks.

3 Melt the butter in a large saucepan. Add the asparagus and onions, cover and cook over a moderate heat for 5–10 minutes or until the vegetables are beginning to soften.

4 Add the stock and parsley, season with salt and pepper and bring to the boil. Cover and simmer for 30 minutes, or until the asparagus and onion are quite tender. Cool slightly.

5 Purée in a blender or food processor until smooth. Sieve if necessary. Cool, then stir in the cream and adjust seasoning. Cover and chill well before serving.

6 Cut six thin slices of brown bread and butter them. Cut off the crusts and halve lengthways. Roll asparagus heads inside each piece of bread; place on a serving plate, cover with cling film and refrigerate until required.

7 Serve the soup well chilled, garnished with wafer thin lemon slices and accompanied by the asparagus rolls.

Chilled Asparagus Soup

CREAM OF LEMON SOUP

SERVES 6

25 g (1 oz) butter or polyunsaturated margarine
2 medium onions, skinned and thinly sliced
75 g (3 oz) carrots, peeled and thinly sliced
75 g (3 oz) celery, washed, trimmed and thinly sliced
2 lemons
1.1 litres (2 pints) stock
2 bay leaves
salt and pepper
150 ml (¼ pint) single cream
spring onion tops or chives and lemon slices, to garnish
pitta bread, to serve

1 Melt the butter or margarine in a large saucepan and add the vegetables. Cover the pan and stew gently for 10–15 minutes until vegetables begin to soften.

Cream of Lemon Soup

2 Meanwhile, thinly pare the lemons using a potato peeler. Blanch the rinds in boiling water for 1 minute; drain. Squeeze the juice from the lemons to give 75–90 ml (5–6 tbsp).

3 Add the rind and juice to the pan with the stock and bay leaves and salt and pepper to taste. Bring to the boil, cover and simmer for 40 minutes or until the carrots and celery are both very soft.

4 Cool the soup a little, remove the bay leaves, then purée the pan contents in a blender or food processor until quite smooth.

5 Return the soup to the rinsed-out pan, reheat gently, stirring in the cream. Do not boil. Adjust seasoning to taste. Serve hot or chilled, garnished with chopped spring onions or chives and lemon slices, and serve with pitta bread.

CAULIFLOWER AND ALMOND CREAM SOUP

SERVES 6

a few saffron strands
60 ml (4 tbsp) boiling water
100 g (4 oz) flaked almonds
50 g (2 oz) butter or polyunsaturated margarine
1 medium onion, skinned and chopped
450 g (1 lb) cauliflower florets
1.3 litres (2¼ pints) stock
freshly grated nutmeg
salt and pepper
150 ml (¼ pint) double cream

1 Soak the saffron in the boiling water for 2 hours. Toast half the almonds on a sheet of foil under the grill, turning them frequently. Leave to cool.

Cauliflower and Almond Cream Soup

2 Melt the butter or margarine in a large saucepan, add the onion and fry gently until soft. Add the cauliflower and the untoasted almonds and stir, cover and cook gently for 10 minutes.

3 Add the stock and stir well, then strain in the yellow saffron liquid. Add a pinch of nutmeg and salt and pepper to taste. Bring to the boil, then lower the heat, cover and simmer for 30 minutes or until the cauliflower is very tender.

4 Purée the soup in a blender or food processor until very smooth. Return to the rinsed-out pan, add half the cream and reheat gently. Taste and adjust seasoning, then pour into a tureen.

5 Swirl in the remaining cream and sprinkle with the toasted almonds and a little nutmeg, if liked. Serve immediately.

CHESTNUT AND ORANGE SOUP

SERVES 6

450 g (1 lb) whole chestnuts
40 g (1½ oz) butter or polyunsaturated margarine
125 g (4 oz) carrots, peeled and finely chopped
2 medium onions, skinned and finely chopped
125 g (4 oz) mushrooms, finely chopped
5 ml (1 tsp) plain wholemeal flour
1.4 litres (2½ pints) stock
salt and pepper
15 ml (1 tbsp) finely grated orange rind

1. Nick the brown outer skins of the chestnuts with a pair of sharp kitchen scissors, or the tip of a sharp knife.

2. Cook the chestnuts in boiling water for 3–5 minutes, then lift out, a few at a time, using a slotted spoon. Peel off both the outer and inner skins and discard.

3. Melt the butter or margarine in a large saucepan, add the vegetables and fry together until lightly browned. Add the flour and cook, stirring, for a further 3–4 minutes or until the flour begins to colour.

4. Remove from the heat and stir in the stock, prepared chestnuts and salt and pepper to taste. Bring slowly to the boil, stirring. Simmer, covered, for 40–45 minutes or until the chestnuts are quite tender.

5. Cool a little, then purée in a blender or food processor, a small quantity at a time. Add half the orange rind and reheat for serving. Adjust seasoning and garnish with the remaining orange rind.

Chestnut and Orange Soup

CARROT AND CARDAMOM SOUP

SERVES 4

200 g (7 oz) carrots, peeled
1 medium onion, skinned
50 g (2 oz) butter or polyunsaturated margarine
10 whole green cardamoms
50 g (2 oz) red lentils, washed
1.1 litres (2 pints) vegetable stock
salt and pepper
parsley sprigs, to garnish

1 Grate the carrots coarsely and slice the onion thinly. Melt the butter or margarine in a large saucepan, add the carrots and onion and cook gently for 4–5 minutes.

Carrot and Cardamom Soup

2 Meanwhile, split each cardamom and remove the black seeds. Crush the seeds with a pestle and mortar, or with the end of a rolling pin.

3 Stir the cardamom seeds into the vegetables with the lentils. Cook, stirring, for a further 1–2 minutes.

4 Add the stock and bring to the boil. Cover and simmer gently for about 20 minutes or until the lentils are just tender. Add salt and pepper to taste before serving and garnish with parsley sprigs. Accompany with chappatis (see page 160) or puris (see page 160), if liked.

VEGETABLE AND OATMEAL BROTH

SERVES 4–6

1 medium onion, skinned
175 g (6 oz) swede, peeled
2 medium carrots, peeled
1 medium leek, trimmed
40 g (1½ oz) butter or polyunsaturated margarine
25 g (1 oz) medium oatmeal
1.1 litres (2 pints) vegetable stock
salt and pepper
150 ml (¼ pint) milk
chopped fresh parsley, to garnish (optional)

1 Dice the onion, swede and carrots finely. Slice the leek in 1 cm (½ inch) rings, then wash well under cold running water to remove any grit.

2 Melt the butter or margarine in a large saucepan, add the vegetables and cook gently without browning for 5 minutes. Add the oatmeal, stir well and cook for a few minutes.

3 Stir in the stock and salt and pepper to taste and bring to the boil. Lower the heat, cover and simmer for about 45 minutes or until tender.

4 Add the milk and reheat to serving temperature. Taste and adjust seasoning before serving sprinkled with chopped parsley, if liked.

CHEESE AND COURGETTE SOUP

SERVES 4

450 g (1 lb) courgettes, trimmed and sliced
1 large onion, skinned and chopped
1 litre (¾ pint) vegetable stock
salt and pepper
175 g (6 oz) garlic and herb cheese
150 ml (¼ pint) single cream
chopped fresh herbs, to garnish

1 Put the courgettes and onion in a large saucepan with the stock. Bring to the boil, then lower the heat, cover the pan and simmer for 20 minutes or until the courgettes are really soft.

2 Sieve or purée the soup in a blender or food processor. Put the cheese in the rinsed-out pan and gradually work in the puréed soup with a wooden spoon.

3 Reheat the soup gently, stirring constantly, then add the cream and heat through without boiling. Taste and adjust seasoning, then pour into 4 warmed soup bowls. Sprinkle with chopped herbs and serve immediately.

Vegetable and Oatmeal Broth

STARTERS

Recipes for vegetarian starters are numerous and apart from soups they vary from salads, mousses, pâtés, soufflés, vegetables and fruit. Always consider what other courses you are serving. If it's a substantial main course then make sure the starter is light and also check that it does not include the same main ingredients. The recipes in this chapter range from Asparagus Mousses, suitable for a special dinner party to Hummus, suitable for an informal supper party. Many of the recipes could equally be served as a light lunch or supper dish.

ASPARAGUS MALTAISE

Serves 6

450 g (1 lb) asparagus, washed and trimmed
3 egg yolks
grated rind and juice of 1 orange
salt and white pepper
100 g (4 oz) unsalted butter, softened
15 ml (1 tbsp) lemon juice
30–45 ml (2–3 tbsp) double cream
orange twists, to garnish

1 Tie the asparagus in bundles of six to eight stalks. Standing them upright in a saucepan of boiling water, cook for 10–15 minutes until tender.

2 Meanwhile, make the sauce. Beat together the egg yolks, orange rind and salt and pepper to taste in a bowl with a knob of the softened butter.

3 Place the bowl over a pan of hot water and whisk in the orange and lemon juice. Cook over a gentle heat and beat in the remaining butter a little at a time.

4 Once the sauce begins to thicken, remove from the heat and continue beating for 1 minute. Adjust seasoning to taste. Stir in the cream.

5 Remove the asparagus from the pan and drain well. Cut and remove the string and garnish with orange twists. Serve immediately with the orange sauce handed separately.

Asparagus Maltaise

STUFFED COURGETTES WITH WALNUTS AND SAGE

Serves 4

4 large courgettes, total weight about 700 g (1½ lb), trimmed
1 medium onion, skinned and chopped
90 g (3½ oz) butter or polyunsaturated margarine
50 g (2 oz) walnut pieces, chopped
50 g (2 oz) fresh wholemeal breadcrumbs
10 ml (2 tsp) chopped fresh sage
15 ml (1 tbsp) tomato purée
1 egg, beaten
salt and pepper
30 ml (2 tbsp) plain wholemeal flour
300 ml (½ pint) stock
30 ml (2 tbsp) chopped fresh parsley
walnut halves and fresh sage sprigs, to garnish

1 Using a fork, score down the courgette skins at 1 cm (½ inch) intervals, then halve each one lengthways.

2 Hollow out the centres of the courgettes using a teaspoon. Blanch in boiling water for 4 minutes, drain, then rinse under cold running water.

3 To make the stuffing, fry the onion in 25 g (1 oz) of the butter or margarine for 5–10 minutes until golden. Remove from heat and stir in half the walnuts, the breadcrumbs, half the sage, the tomato purée, beaten egg and salt and pepper to taste. Sandwich the courgettes with the stuffing.

4 Place in a greased ovenproof dish and dot with a little more butter or margarine. Cover and bake at 190°C (375°F) mark 5 for about 30 minutes.

5 Meanwhile, make the sauce. Melt 50 g (2 oz) of the butter or margarine in a pan, stir in the flour and cook gently for 1 minute, stirring.

6 Remove from the heat and gradually add the stock. Bring to the boil and continue to cook, stirring until the sauce thickens. Stir in the parsley, salt and pepper to taste, with the remaining sage and walnuts. Remove from heat and cover.

7 To serve, reheat the sauce. Pour some over the courgettes and serve the rest separately. Garnish with walnut halves and sage sprigs.

BLUE CHEESE CROQUETTES

Serves 4–6

100 g (4 oz) celery, washed and trimmed
75 g (3 oz) butter or polyunsaturated margarine
75 g (3 oz) plain wholemeal flour, plus a little extra for coating
225 ml (8 fl oz) milk
175 g (6 oz) Blue Stilton cheese, grated
30 ml (2 tbsp) snipped fresh chives or 15 ml (1 tbsp) dried
2 eggs
pepper
65 g (2½ oz) dried wholemeal breadcrumbs
polyunsaturated oil, for deep frying

1 Finely chop the celery; fry in the butter or margarine for 5–10 minutes until beginning to become brown.

2 Stir in the flour; cook for 1 minute. Off the heat, stir in the milk. Bring to the boil, stirring, then cook for 1 minute – the mixture will be *very* thick.

3 Remove from the heat and stir in the grated cheese, chives, one egg and pepper (the cheese will add sufficient salt).

4 Spread out the mixture in a shallow dish, cover with damp greaseproof paper and cool for 30 minutes. Refrigerate for 2–3 hours to firm up.

5 Shape the mixture into twelve croquettes, then coat lightly in flour, beaten egg and breadcrumbs.

6 Deep fry the croquettes at 180°C (350°F), a few at a time, for 3–4 minutes until golden brown. Serve hot.

MARINATED MUSHROOMS

SERVES 4

450 g (1 lb) small button mushrooms
30 ml (2 tbsp) wine vinegar
90 ml (6 tbsp) polyunsaturated oil
pinch of mustard powder
pinch of raw cane sugar
salt and pepper
chopped fresh parsley, to garnish

1 Trim the mushrooms. Leave small mushrooms whole and cut larger ones into quarters.

Marinated Mushrooms

2 Put the vinegar, oil, mustard and sugar in a bowl with salt and pepper to taste. Whisk together with a fork until well blended.

3 Add the mushrooms and stir to coat in the marinade. Cover and leave to marinate in the refrigerator for 6–8 hours, stirring occasionally.

4 Taste and adjust the seasoning of the mushrooms, then divide equally between 4 individual shallow serving dishes. Sprinkle with chopped parsley and serve immediately. Accompany with crusty brown bread, if liked.

NUTTY CAMEMBERT PÂTÉ

Serves 4–6

175 g (6 oz) soft ripe Camembert cheese
225 g (8 oz) full-fat soft cheese
2.5 ml (½ tsp) paprika
salt and pepper
75 g (3 oz) finely chopped blanched almonds
extra paprika, to serve

1. Cut the rind off the Camembert, then work the cheese through a sieve into a bowl, or work in a blender or food processor until smooth.

2. Add the soft cheese, paprika and salt and pepper to taste. Beat vigorously with a wooden spoon to combine the ingredients well.

3. Spoon the pâté into a greased and base-lined 300 ml (½ pint) dish or mould. Press down well and smooth the surface with the back of the spoon. Cover the dish and freeze for 1 hour.

4. Loosen the pâté from the dish by running a palette knife between the two. Turn the pâté out upside down on to a serving plate and peel off the lining paper. Chill overnight.

5. Sprinkle the nuts over the pâté, then press evenly over the top and around the sides with the palette knife. Sprinkle with paprika. Serve chilled. Accompany with wholemeal toast, if liked.

Nutty Camembert Pâté

ARTICHOKE HEARTS À LA GRÈCQUE

SERVES 6

75 ml (5 tbsp) olive oil
15 ml (1 tbsp) white wine vinegar
10 ml (2 tsp) tomato purée
1 large garlic clove, skinned and crushed
7.5 ml (1½ tsp) chopped fresh thyme or basil
salt and pepper
175 g (6 oz) button onions, skinned
5 ml (1 tsp) raw cane sugar
225 g (8 oz) small button mushrooms
two 400 g (14 oz) cans artichoke hearts

1 Make the dressing. Put 45 ml (3 tbsp) olive oil, vinegar, tomato purée, garlic, thyme and salt and pepper to taste in a bowl and whisk together.

2 Blanch the onions in boiling water for 5 minutes; drain well. Heat remaining oil, add onions and sugar and cook for 2 minutes.

3 Add the mushrooms and toss over a high heat for a few seconds. Tip contents of pan into the dressing. Drain artichoke hearts, rinse and dry. Add hearts to dressing and toss together. Cover and chill until ready to serve.

FETA, AVOCADO AND TOMATO SALAD

SERVES 4

2 ripe avocados
120 ml (8 tbsp) French dressing (see page 155)
4 medium tomatoes
50 g (2 oz) black olives or green stuffed olives
225 g (8 oz) Feta cheese
30 ml (2 tbsp) chopped fresh marjoram

1 Halve the avocados lengthways and remove the stones; then peel and cut the avocados into slices.

2 Pour the vinaigrette over the avocado slices. Stir gently to coat the slices thoroughly.

3 Cut each tomato into eight. Stone the black olives, if used, and dice the cheese.

4 Arrange the avocados, tomatoes, olives and cheese in a salad bowl. Spoon over the dressing and sprinkle with chopped marjoram to serve.

PEPERONATA
(Sweet Pepper and Tomato Stew)

SERVES 6

75 ml (5 tbsp) olive oil
1 large onion, skinned and finely sliced
6 red peppers, cored and seeded
2 garlic cloves, skinned and crushed
700 g (1½ lb) ripe tomatoes, skinned and roughly chopped
15 ml (1 tbsp) chopped fresh parsley
salt and pepper

1 Heat the oil in a frying pan, add the onion and fry gently for 5 minutes until soft but not coloured.

2 Slice the peppers into strips and add to the pan with the garlic. Cook gently for 2–3 minutes, then add the tomatoes, parsley and salt and pepper to taste.

3 Cover and cook gently for 30 minutes until the mixture is quite dry: if necessary, remove the lid 10 minutes before the end of cooking to allow the liquid to evaporate. Taste and adjust seasoning. Chill before serving.

Peperonata

MOZZARELLA-STUFFED TOMATOES

Serves 4

4 large, firm tomatoes
salt and pepper
50 g (2 oz) black olives
225 g (8 oz) Mozzarella cheese, grated
1–2 garlic cloves, skinned and crushed
20 ml (4 tsp) chopped fresh basil or 10 ml (2 tsp) dried
135 ml (9 tbsp) olive oil
45 ml (3 tbsp) lemon juice
fresh basil sprigs, to garnish

1 Skin each tomato by piercing the stalk end with a fork and holding over a gas flame or under the grill. Turn the tomato until the skin bursts. Leave until cool enough to handle, then peel off the skin.

2 Cut a slice off the rounded end of each tomato and reserve. Scoop out the insides of the tomatoes with a teaspoon. Sprinkle the insides with salt and stand cut side down on absorbent kitchen paper.

3 Reserve four whole black olives, then stone and chop the remainder. Put the Mozzarella in a bowl with the chopped olives, garlic and half the basil. Mix well, then add salt and pepper to taste. (Add salt sparingly as olives tend to be salty.)

4 Place the tomatoes in a serving dish and spoon in the Mozzarella mixture. Replace the reserved tomato slices at an angle so that the Mozzarella filling is visible.

5 Whisk together the oil and lemon juice with the remaining basil and salt and pepper to taste. Pour over the tomatoes, then chill for at least 2 hours, spooning the dressing over from time to time. Serve chilled, garnished with the whole olives and basil sprigs.

Mozzarella-Stuffed Tomatoes

AVOCADO AND KIWI FRUIT VINAIGRETTE

Serves 8

1 egg
150 ml (1/4 pint) olive oil
60 ml (4 tbsp) white wine vinegar
45 ml (3 tbsp) chopped fresh parsley
salt and pepper
4 kiwi fruit
3 small ripe avocados
watercress sprigs, to garnish
wholemeal French-style bread, to serve

1 Boil the egg for 6 minutes only. Meanwhile, whisk together the oil, vinegar, parsley and salt and pepper to taste in a medium bowl.

2 Run cold water over the boiled egg to cool. Shell and halve the egg. Scoop out the yolk into the dressing. Chop the egg white finely and add to the dressing, whisking well to ensure it is evenly mixed.

3 Peel the kiwi fruit and slice it into rings, discarding the ends. Stir into the dressing, cover and refrigerate for at least 2 hours.

4 Halve, peel and slice the avocados and arrange on individual serving plates together with the drained kiwi fruit slices.

5 Spoon the dressing over the avocados and kiwi fruit and garnish with watercress sprigs. Serve with wholemeal French-style bread.

CELERIAC RÉMOULADE

SERVES 6

1 large head celeriac
30 ml (2 tbsp) lemon juice
300 ml (½ pint) mayonnaise (see page 154)
30 ml (2 tbsp) snipped fresh chives
30 ml (2 tbsp) French mustard
salt and pepper
1 lettuce or curly endive
chopped fresh parsley, to garnish

1. Peel and coarsely grate the celeriac. Toss immediately in the lemon juice to prevent discoloration.

2. Add the mayonnaise, chives and mustard with salt and pepper to taste and mix well together.

3. Line individual dishes or plates with lettuce, then pile the celeriac mixture in the centre. Sprinkle with chopped parsley and serve immediately.

Celeriac Rémoulade

AUBERGINE AND CHEESE SOUFFLÉ

SERVES 4

450 g (1 lb) aubergines
salt and pepper
75 g (3 oz) butter or polyunsaturated margarine
30 ml (2 tbsp) plain wholemeal flour
150 ml (¼ pint) milk
100 g (4 oz) Red Leicester or Cheddar cheese, grated
4 eggs, separated
40 g (1½ oz) grated Parmesan cheese

1 Chop the aubergines roughly and place in a colander or sieve. Sprinkle liberally with salt and set aside to drain for 30 minutes. Rinse under cold running water, then pat dry with absorbent kitchen paper.

2 Melt 50 g (2 oz) of the butter or margarine in a saucepan and add the aubergines. Cover and cook gently until golden brown and completely soft. Purée in a blender or food processor until nearly smooth.

3 Melt the remaining butter or margarine in a clean saucepan, add the flour and cook over low heat, stirring with a wooden spoon, for 2 minutes. Remove the pan from the heat and gradually blend in the milk, stirring after each addition to prevent lumps forming. Bring to the boil slowly, then simmer for 2–3 minutes, stirring.

4 Remove from the heat and stir in the aubergine purée, the Red Leicester or Cheddar cheese, the egg yolks and salt and pepper to taste. Turn into a bowl, cover and chill until required.

5 Lightly grease a 1.4 litre (2½ pint) soufflé dish and dust with all but 25 g (1 oz) of the Parmesan cheese.

6 Whisk the egg whites until stiff but not dry. Fold into the aubergine mixture until evenly combined. Spoon into the prepared dish and sprinkle with the remaining Parmesan. Bake at 200°C (400°F) mark 6 for 25–30 minutes. Serve immediately.

IMAM BAYILDI
(Cold Stuffed Baked Aubergine)

SERVES 6

6 long, small aubergines
salt and pepper
200 ml (7 fl oz) olive oil
450 g (1 lb) onions, skinned and finely sliced
3 garlic cloves, skinned and crushed
397 g (14 oz) can tomatoes, drained or 450 g (1 lb) tomatoes, skinned, seeded and chopped
60 ml (4 tbsp) chopped fresh parsley, plus extra to garnish
3.75 ml (¾ tsp) ground allspice
5 ml (1 tsp) raw cane sugar
30 ml (2 tbsp) lemon juice

1 Halve the aubergines lengthways. Scoop out, leaving a substantial shell so they do not disintegrate, and reserve flesh. Sprinkle the insides of the shells with salt and invert on a plate for 30 minutes to drain any bitter juices.

2 Heat 45 ml (3 tbsp) of the olive oil in a saucepan, add the onion and garlic and fry gently for about 15 minutes until soft but not coloured. Add the tomatoes, aubergine flesh, parsley, allspice and salt and pepper to taste. Simmer gently for about 20 minutes until the mixture has reduced and thickened.

3 Rinse the aubergines and dry with absorbent kitchen paper. Spoon the filling into each half and place side by side, quite closely, in a shallow ovenproof dish.

4 Mix the remaining oil with 150 ml (¼ pint) water, the sugar, lemon juice and salt and pepper to taste. Pour around the aubergines, cover and bake at 150°C (300°F) mark 2 for at least 1 hour until completely tender.

5 Remove from the oven, uncover and leave to cool for 1 hour. Chill for at least 2 hours before serving garnished with lots of chopped parsley. Accompany with wholemeal bread, if liked.

Imam Bayildi (Cold stuffed baked aubergine)

SALADES RÂPÉES CRUES
(Grated Raw Vegetables with Garlic Dressing)

SERVES 4

175 g (6 oz) carrots, peeled
175 g (6 oz) courgettes, trimmed
175 g (6 oz) celeriac
15 ml (1 tbsp) lemon juice
175 g (6 oz) raw beetroot
90 ml (6 tbsp) olive oil
30 ml (2 tbsp) wine vinegar
2.5 ml (½ tsp) raw cane sugar
2.5 ml (½ tsp) mustard
1 garlic clove, skinned and crushed
salt and pepper
chopped fresh parsley, to garnish

1 Grate the carrots, avoiding the central core. Grate the courgettes and mix with the carrots, in a salad bowl.

2 Peel and grate the celeriac, toss immediately in the lemon juice and add to the carrot and courgette mixture. Lastly, peel and grate the beetroot and add to the mixture.

3 Put the oil, vinegar, sugar, mustard and garlic in a screw-top jar with salt and pepper to taste. Shake the jar until the dressing is emulsified.

4 Pour the dressing over the vegetables and toss lightly just to coat. Serve immediately garnished with chopped parsley.

HUMMUS

SERVES 8

225 g (8 oz) dried chick peas, soaked in cold water overnight, or two 400 g (14 oz) cans chick peas
juice of 2 large lemons
150 ml (¼ pint) tahini (paste of finely ground sesame seeds)
60 ml (4 tbsp) olive oil
1–2 garlic cloves, skinned and crushed
salt and pepper
black olives and chopped fresh parsley, to garnish
warm pitta bread, to serve

1 If using dried chick peas, drain, place in a saucepan and cover with cold water. Bring to the boil and simmer gently for 2 hours or until tender.

2 Drain the peas, reserving a little of the liquid. Put them in a blender or food processor, reserving a few for garnish, and gradually add the reserved liquid and the lemon juice, blending well after each addition to form a smooth purée.

3 Add the tahini paste, oil (reserving 10 ml/2 tsp) and garlic and salt and pepper to taste. Blend again until smooth.

4 Spoon into a serving dish and sprinkle with the reserved oil. Garnish with the reserved chick peas, and the olives and chopped parsley. Serve with warm pitta bread.

FETA CHEESE SOUFFLÉ

SERVES 6

grated Parmesan cheese
25 g (1 oz) butter or polyunsaturated margarine
30 ml (2 tbsp) plain wholemeal flour
200 ml (7 fl oz) milk
salt and pepper
225 g (8 oz) Feta cheese, grated
50 g (2 oz) stuffed olives, chopped
4 eggs, separated

1 Grease a 1.7 litre (3 pint) soufflé dish and dust with the grated Parmesan.

2 Melt the butter or margarine in a saucepan, add the flour and cook for 1 minute, stirring. Off the heat, gradually stir in the milk and pepper. Bring to the boil and cook for 2–3 minutes, stirring. Allow to cool slightly, then beat in the Feta, olives and egg yolks. Season with salt and pepper to taste.

3 Whisk the egg whites until stiff and beat a large spoonful into the sauce. Lightly fold in the rest and pour the mixture into the dish.

4 Bake at 180°C (350°F) mark 4 for about 40 minutes or until the soufflé is golden. Serve immediately.

ARTICHOKES WITH HOLLANDAISE SAUCE

SERVES 4

4 globe artichokes
½ lemon
300 ml (½ pint) hollandaise sauce *(see page 187)*

1 Break off the toughest outer leaves from each artichoke. With a sharp knife, cut off the stem quite close to the base leaves.

2 Trim the spiky leaf tops, according to variety, with a sharp knife or scissors. Rub the cut surfaces with the lemon half to prevent discoloration.

3 Globe artichokes have close-fisted leaves which make havens for insects, particularly earwigs. Wash them well under running water or soak the whole artichokes in a bowl of cold water for about 30 minutes.

4 Place the artichokes in a large saucepan of boiling salted water. Simmer gently for 35–40 minutes, according to size. To test whether the artichoke is cooked, try pulling out a leaf. If it comes out easily, the artichoke is cooked. Turn the heads upside down in a colander to drain for a few minutes.

5 The 'choke' must never be eaten as the little barbs can irritate the throat. You can easily recognise the choke: it is a mass of yellowish silky hairs arising out of the firm-textured heart. To remove the chokes, carefully peel back the leaves until it is exposed then scoop them out with a spoon. Serve the artichokes while still hot, with the warm hollandaise sauce.

MEXICAN AVOCADO DIP

SERVES 6

30 ml (2 tbsp) polyunsaturated oil
1 small onion, skinned and finely chopped
2 garlic cloves, skinned and crushed
2.5 ml (½ tsp) chilli powder
4 tomatoes, skinned and chopped
2 ripe avocados
juice of ½ lemon
150 ml (¼ pint) soured cream
salt and pepper
tomato slices, to garnish

1 Heat the oil in a small pan, add the onion, garlic and chilli and fry gently, stirring, until onion is soft. Add the tomatoes and fry for a further 5 minutes, breaking them up with a wooden spoon.

2 Put the tomato mixture into a blender or food processor and blend until smooth. Turn into a bowl and leave to cool.

3 Halve and stone the avocados. Peel three halves, add to the tomato mixture with the lemon juice and mash to a purée. Blend in half the soured cream, then taste and add salt and pepper and more chilli powder, if liked.

4 Transfer the dip to a shallow serving bowl. Peel and slice the remaining avocado half. Arrange avocado slices on top of dip, alternating with tomato slices.

5 To serve, spoon the remaining cream into the centre and sprinkle with a little chilli powder. Serve immediately.

Mexican Avocado Dip

ASPARAGUS MOUSSES

Serves 6

700 g (1½ lb) fresh asparagus
50 g (2 oz) butter
1 medium onion, skinned and finely chopped
30 ml (2 tbsp) lemon juice
150 ml (¼ pint) double cream
3 egg yolks
salt and pepper
1 egg white

1 Cut the heads off the asparagus to a length of about 4 cm (1½ inches) and reserve. Slice the stalks into 1 cm (½ inch) lengths, discarding any tough root ends.

2 Melt the butter in a medium saucepan. Add the asparagus stalks, onion and lemon juice, then pour in 200 ml (7 fl oz) water. Cover tightly and cook gently for about 30 minutes or until the asparagus is tender.

3 Drain well, then put in a blender or food processor with the cream. Work until almost smooth.

4 Rub the purée through a nylon sieve into a bowl to remove any stringy particles. Beat in the egg yolks with salt and pepper to taste. Whisk the egg white until stiff and fold into the asparagus mixture.

5 Spoon the asparagus mixture into six 150 ml (¼ pint) ramekins, then stand the dishes in a roasting tin. Pour in enough hot water to come half way up the sides of the ramekins.

6 Bake the mousses at 170°C (325°F) mark 3 for 40–45 minutes or until just firm when pressed lightly in the centres. Ten minutes before the end of cooking time, cook the asparagus heads in a steamer for 5–10 minutes until tender.

7 Serve the mousses immediately, topped with the asparagus heads. Accompany with thin slices of wholemeal toast, if liked.

Asparagus Mousses

BROCCOLI FRITTERS

SERVES 4

900 g (2 lb) fresh broccoli
plain wholemeal flour, for dusting
salt and pepper
150 ml (¼ pint) fritter batter (see page 185)
polyunsaturated oil, for deep frying
300 ml (½ pint) quick tomato sauce (see page 187), to serve

1. Trim off and discard the thick ends of the broccoli, then cut into large florets. Cook in boiling salted water for about 10 minutes until nearly tender. Drain the broccoli well.

2. Dust with flour seasoned with salt and pepper. Lightly turn the broccoli in the batter, using a spoon and fork to coat evenly. Heat the oil in a deep-fat frier to 180°C (350°F). Deep fry in batches for 1–2 minutes until golden.

3. With a slotted spoon, transfer the fritters to a wire rack. Keep warm in a cool oven, uncovered, while cooking the remainder. Serve immediately with hot tomato sauce.

VARIATIONS

AUBERGINE FRITTERS
Cut 2 aubergines into 1 cm (½ inch) slices. Blanch for 1 minute in boiling salted water, drain well and proceed as from step 2.

CARROT FRITTERS
Cut 900 g (2 lb) carrots into finger-sized sticks. Do not blanch, but proceed as from step 2.

MUSHROOM FRITTERS
Wipe 450 g (1 lb) button mushrooms and proceed as from step 2.

COURGETTE FRITTERS
Cut 900 g (2 lb) courgettes into 1 cm (½ inch) slices. Blanch for 1 minute in boiling salted water, drain well and proceed as from step 2.

BUTTER BEAN PÂTÉ

SERVES 6–8

225 g (8 oz) dried butter beans, soaked in cold water overnight or two 396 g (14 oz) cans butter beans
60 ml (4 tbsp) olive oil
juice of 2 lemons
2 garlic cloves, skinned and crushed
30 ml (2 tbsp) chopped fresh coriander
salt and pepper
coriander sprigs and black olives, to garnish

1. Drain the dried butter beans into a sieve and rinse thoroughly under cold running water. Put in a saucepan, cover with cold water and bring to the boil.

2. With a slotted spoon, skim off any scum that rises to the surface. Half cover the pan with a lid and simmer for 1½–2 hours until the beans are very tender.

3. Drain the dried or canned beans and rinse under cold running water. Put half of the beans in a blender or food processor with half of the oil, lemon juice, garlic and coriander. Blend to a smooth purée, then transfer to a bowl. Repeat with the remaining beans, oil, lemon juice, garlic and coriander.

4. Beat the 2 batches of purée together until well mixed, then add salt and pepper to taste.

5. Turn the pâté into a serving bowl and rough up the surface with the prongs of a fork. Garnish with the coriander and black olives. Chill until serving time. Accompany with fingers of hot wholemeal pitta bread or granary toast, if liked.

Butter Bean Pâté

MELON WITH PORT

SERVES 4

2 small Charentais, Cantaloupe or Ogen melons
180 ml (12 tbsp) port
mint sprigs, to garnish

1 Halve the melons horizontally, trimming the bases so they will stand firmly. Scoop out the seeds with a teaspoon and discard.

2 Pour 45 ml (3 tbsp) of port into each half. Cover with cling film and chill for at least 1 hour. Serve garnished with mint sprigs.

AUBERGINE SAMOSAS

SERVES 4

1 small aubergine, about 225 g (8 oz)
salt and pepper
15 ml (1 tbsp) polyunsaturated oil, plus extra for deep frying
1 garlic clove, skinned and crushed
1.25 ml (¼ tsp) ground allspice
2 tomatoes, skinned and chopped
30 ml (2 tbsp) chopped fresh coriander
125 g (4 oz) wholemeal pastry (see page 183)

1 Chop the aubergine finely. Place in a colander, sprinkling each layer with salt. Cover with a plate, place heavy weights on top and leave for 30 minutes, then rinse well under cold running water and dry with absorbent kitchen paper.

2 Heat the oil in a heavy-based saucepan, add the aubergine, garlic and allspice and fry gently for 5–7 minutes or until softened. Stir in the tomatoes and coriander. Season with pepper only, then remove from the heat and leave to cool for 15–20 minutes.

3 Roll out the pastry thinly on a well-floured surface. Stamp out eight 10 cm (4 inch) rounds. Spoon a little filling on each, brush the pastry edges with water and fold over to form semi-circular shapes. Press the edges well together. Place on a plate, cover loosely and chill for 30 minutes.

4 Heat the oil in a deep-fat frier to 180°C (350°F). Deep fry the samosas in batches for 4–5 minutes until golden. Drain well and serve immediately.

Melon with Port

LUNCHES, SUPPERS AND SNACKS

Most vegetarians eat eggs and cheese and many of the recipes here are based on these ingredients. Both are a good source of protein and make ideal light dishes. Most hard cheeses are made with rennet which is derived from an animal source and are therefore not strictly vegetarian. There are, however, other cheeses available which are made from vegetable rennet and these are ideal for strict vegetarians. Many of the dishes here can be served on their own or simply with wholemeal bread or a baked potato for a nutritious dish. Several, such as Falafel (Israeli Chick Pea Patties) or Aubergine Dip, could equally be served as a starter.

TAGLIATELLE WITH CHEESE AND NUT SAUCE

SERVES 4

400 g (14 oz) wholewheat or green (spinach) tagliatelle
salt and pepper
100 g (4 oz) Gorgonzola cheese
100 g (4 oz) walnuts, chopped
5 ml (1 tsp) chopped fresh sage or 2.5 ml (½ tsp) dried
75 ml (5 tbsp) olive oil
15 ml (1 tbsp) chopped fresh parsley, to garnish

1 Plunge the tagliatelle into a large saucepan of boiling salted water. Simmer, uncovered, for 10 minutes or according to packet instructions, until *al dente* (tender but firm to the bite).

2 Meanwhile, crumble the cheese into a blender or food processor. Add two-thirds of the walnuts and the sage. Blend to combine the ingredients.

3 Add the oil gradually through the funnel (as when making mayonnaise) and blend until the sauce is evenly incorporated.

4 Drain the tagliatelle well and return to the pan. Add the nut sauce and fold in gently to mix. Add salt and pepper to taste.

5 Transfer to a warmed serving bowl and sprinkle with the remaining walnuts. Serve immediately garnished with chopped parsley.

Tagliatelle with Cheese and Nut Sauce

PIZZA-IN-THE-PAN

Serves 2

225 g (8 oz) self-raising wholemeal flour
salt and pepper
60 ml (4 tbsp) polyunsaturated oil
75 ml (5 tbsp) tomato purée
397 g (14 oz) can tomatoes, drained and chopped
175 g (6 oz) Cheddar cheese, grated
chopped fresh herbs
a few black olives

1 Put the flour and salt and pepper into a bowl. Make a well in the centre and pour in 30 ml (2 tbsp) of the oil and 60 ml (4 tbsp) water. Mix to a soft dough – you will find that it binds together very quickly, although you may need to add a little more water.

2 Knead the dough lightly on a floured surface, then roll out to a circle to fit a medium-sized frying pan.

3 Heat half the remaining oil in the pan. Add the circle of dough and fry gently for about 5 minutes until the base is cooked and lightly browned.

4 Turn the dough out onto a plate and flip it over.

5 Heat the remaining oil in the pan, then slide the dough back into the pan, browned side uppermost. Spread with the tomato purée, then top with the tomatoes and sprinkle over grated cheese, herbs and black olives.

6 Cook for a further 5 minutes until the underside is done, then slide the pan under a preheated grill. Cook for 3–4 minutes until the cheese melts. Serve immediately.

LOVAGE AND BLUE CHEESE OMELETTE

Serves 2

4 eggs
10 ml (2 tsp) chopped fresh lovage
salt and pepper
75 g (3 oz) Blue Cheshire or Stilton cheese
15 g (½ oz) butter or polyunsaturated margarine
lovage leaves, to garnish

1 Whisk together the eggs, lovage, 30 ml (2 tbsp) water and salt and pepper to taste. Grate the cheese coarsely, or cut it into thin slivers and set aside.

2 Heat the butter or margarine in a 20.5 cm (8 inch) non-stick frying pan. When foaming, pour in the egg mixture all at once.

3 Cook over a moderate-high heat for a few minutes, drawing a fork through the omelette to allow the unset egg mixture to run through to the edges.

4 When set underneath but still creamy on top, scatter the cheese over the surface of the omelette. Leave for a few moments until the cheese starts to melt, then fold over the omelette into three.

5 To serve, slide on to a serving plate. Garnish with lovage leaves. Divide in two for serving.

Lovage and Blue Cheese Omelette

FRIED POLENTA STICKS

SERVES 4

10 ml (2 tsp) salt
225 g (8 oz) coarse-grain cornmeal or polenta flour
polyunsaturated oil, for frying
250–350 g (8–12 oz) Torta San Gaudenzio or Fontina cheese, to serve
tomato sauce, to serve (see page 187)

1 To make the polenta sticks, put 1 litre (1¾ pints) water and the salt in a large pan and bring to simmering point.

2 Add the cornmeal in a very fine stream, stirring vigorously all the time with a long-handled wooden spoon. (Do not add the cornmeal all at once or it will become hard.)

3 When the mixture is smooth and thick, simmer for 20–30 minutes, stirring, until polenta comes away from sides of pan.

4 Turn on a wooden board and shape it into a cake about 5 cm (2 inches) high with a dampened wooden spoon. Leave for about 1 hour to cool.

5 When cold, divide the polenta into four sections, then cut each of the sections into 2.5 cm (1 inch) sticks.

6 Heat enough oil in a frying pan to come 2.5 cm (1 inch) up the sides of the pan. Fry the polenta sticks in batches for about 3 minutes on each side until crisp. Drain on absorbent kitchen paper and serve hot, with slices of the cheese and the tomato sauce handed separately.

Fried Polenta Sticks

CAULIFLOWER AND COURGETTE TARTLETS

MAKES 6

75 ml (5 tbsp) dry white wine
30 ml (2 tbsp) polyunsaturated oil
5 ml (1 tsp) chopped fresh tarragon or 1.25 ml (¼ tsp) dried
1 garlic clove, skinned and crushed
salt and pepper
225 g (8 oz) cauliflower, trimmed and cut into small florets
175 g (6 oz) small courgettes, trimmed
150 g (6 oz) plain wholemeal flour
75 g (3 oz) butter or polyunsaturated margarine

1 To make the dressing, in a medium bowl, whisk together the wine, oil, tarragon, crushed garlic and salt and pepper to taste.

2 Blanch the cauliflower florets in boiling salted water for 1 minute only. Drain well, and while still hot stir into the dressing.

3 Slice the courgettes into thin rings and add to the bowl, stirring gently to mix. Leave to cool, then cover with cling film and refrigerate for several hours or overnight.

4 Make the pastry. Add a pinch of salt to the flour and rub in the butter or margarine until the mixture resembles fine breadcrumbs. Bind to a dough with 15–30 ml (1–2 tbsp) water.

5 Knead the pastry lightly until just smooth, then roll out and use to line six 7.5 cm (3 inch) flan tins. Prick the bases with a fork, then line with foil and baking beans.

6 Bake blind at 200°C (400°F) mark 6 for about 15 minutes or until just set and tinged with colour. Remove the paper and baking beans and return to the oven for a further 8–10 minutes or until well browned.

7 Cool slightly, ease cases out of tins and leave for 2 hours until completely cold. Store in an airtight container until required.

8 Just before serving, place the pastry cases on individual plates and spoon in the cauliflower and courgette salad.

BAKED POTATOES WITH CHICK PEAS

SERVES 4

4 baking potatoes, about 275 g (10 oz) each
45 ml (3 tbsp) polyunsaturated oil
salt and pepper
1 medium onion, skinned and roughly chopped
2.5 ml (½ tsp) ground coriander
2.5 ml (½ tsp) ground cumin
400 g (14 oz) can chick peas, drained
60 ml (4 tbsp) chopped fresh parsley
150 ml (¼ pint) natural yogurt
chopped fresh parsley, to garnish

1 Scrub the potatoes under cold running water and pat dry with absorbent kitchen paper. Brush with 15 ml (1 tbsp) of the oil and sprinkle with salt.

2 Run thin skewers through the potatoes to help conduct the heat. Put them directly on the oven shelves and bake at 200°C (400°F) mark 6 for 1¼ hours until tender.

Baked Potatoes with Chick Peas

3 Meanwhile, heat remaining oil in a large saucepan, add the onion, coriander and cumin and fry for 4 minutes, stirring occasionally. Add the chick peas and cook for 1–2 minutes, stirring all the time.

4 Halve the potatoes and scoop out the flesh, keeping the shells intact. Add the potato flesh to the chick pea mixture with the parsley and yogurt. Mash until smooth and add salt and pepper to taste.

5 Place the potato shells on a baking sheet and fill with the potato and chick pea mixture. Return to the oven and bake for a further 10–15 minutes. Serve hot, sprinkled with chopped parsley.

FALAFEL
(Israeli Chick Pea Patties)

SERVES 4–6

225 g (8 oz) chick peas, soaked in cold water overnight
1 medium onion, skinned and roughly chopped
1 garlic clove, skinned and roughly chopped
10 ml (2 tsp) ground cumin
30 ml (2 tbsp) chopped fresh coriander or 5 ml (1 tsp) dried
1.25 ml (¼ tsp) chilli powder
5 ml (1 tsp) salt
pepper
plain wholemeal flour, for coating
1 egg, beaten
polyunsaturated oil, for deep frying

1 Drain the chick peas and rinse well under cold running water. Put in a large saucepan, cover with plenty of fresh cold water and bring slowly to the boil. Skim off any scum with a slotted spoon, then half cover with a lid and simmer for 1 hour or until tender.

2 Drain the chick peas thoroughly and put in a blender or food processor. Add the onion, garlic, cumin, coriander, chilli powder and salt. Work the mixture until smooth.

3 With floured hands, shape the mixture into about 20 small flat cakes. Dip them 1 at a time in the beaten egg, then coat them in more flour seasoned with salt and pepper. Chill for at least 1 hour.

4 Pour enough oil into a deep frying pan to come about 2.5 cm (1 inch) up the sides. Heat until very hot, then fry the falafel in batches for about 3 minutes on each side until golden, turning once. Drain on absorbent kitchen paper. Serve hot or cold in pitta bread with salad or a dip such as natural yogurt, if liked.

PASTA SHELLS WITH CHEESE AND WALNUTS

SERVES 4

275 g (10 oz) pasta shells or other pasta shapes
salt and pepper
25 g (1 oz) butter or polyunsaturated margarine
225 g (8 oz) Mascarpone or other full-fat soft cheese
30 ml (2 tbsp) freshly grated Parmesan cheese
75 g (3 oz) walnuts, roughly chopped

1 Cook the pasta in a large pan of boiling salted water for 20 minutes or until just tender. Drain well.

2 In the same pan, melt the butter or margarine, add the soft cheese and stir for about 2–3 minutes until heated through. Do not boil.

3 Add the Parmesan and walnuts, stir, then add the pasta. Mix well until evenly coated with sauce. Season with salt and pepper to taste. Serve immediately.

Pasta Shells with Cheese and Walnuts

RAVIOLI
(Pasta Filled with Ricotta and Spinach)

SERVES 4

350 g (12 oz) washed fresh spinach or 175 g (6 oz) frozen
175 g (6 oz) Ricotta or curd cheese
115 g (4½ oz) freshly grated Parmesan
1 egg, beaten
pinch of freshly grated nutmeg or ground allspice
salt and pepper
basic pasta dough made with 3 eggs and 300 g (11 oz) plain wholemeal flour (see page 184)
75 g (3 oz) butter or polyunsaturated margarine
a few fresh sage leaves, chopped, and a few extra, to garnish

1 Make the pasta stuffing. Put the spinach in a saucepan without any water and cook gently for 5–10 minutes, or until thawed if using frozen spinach. Drain very well and chop the spinach finely.

2 Mix together the spinach, Ricotta or curd cheese, 65 g (2½ oz) Parmesan, the egg, nutmeg and salt and pepper to taste.

3 Cut the dough in two. Wrap one half in cling film. Pat the other half out to a rectangle, then roll out firmly to an even sheet of almost paper-thin pasta. If pasta sticks, ease it carefully and flour lightly underneath. Make sure there are no holes or creases. Cover with a clean damp cloth and repeat with other half of dough.

4 Working quickly to prevent the pasta drying out, place teaspoonfuls of the filling evenly spaced at 4 cm (1½ inch) intervals across and down the sheet of dough that has just been rolled out and is not covered.

5 With a pastry brush or your index finger, glaze the spaces between the filling with beaten egg or water – this acts as a bond to seal the ravioli.

6 Uncover the other sheet of pasta, carefully lift this on the rolling-pin (to avoid stretching) and unroll it over the first sheet, easing gently. Press down firmly around the pockets of filling and along the dampened lines to push out any trapped air and seal well.

7 With a ravioli cutter, serrated edged wheel or even a sharp knife, cut the ravioli into squares between the pouches. Lift the ravioli one by one on to a well-floured baking sheet and leave to dry for about 1 hour before cooling (or cover with cling film and refrigerate overnight).

8 Pour at least 2.3 litres (4 pints) water into a pan and bring to the boil. Add 10 ml (2 tsp) salt.

9 Add the ravioli a few at a time, stirring so that they do not stick together. (A few drops of oil added to the water will stop it boiling over.) Cook the ravioli at a gentle boil for about 5 minutes until just tender. Remove with a slotted spoon and place in a warmed greased serving dish. Keep hot while cooking the remainder of the ravioli.

10 Melt the butter or margarine in a saucepan and stir in the rest of the grated Parmesan cheese with the chopped sage. Pour over the ravioli and toss to coat evenly. Serve immediately, garnished with fresh sage.

CURRIED EGGS

SERVES 4

30 ml (2 tbsp) polyunsaturated oil
1 medium onion, skinned and chopped
1 medium cooking apple, peeled, cored and chopped
10 ml (2 tsp) garam masala
300 ml (½ pint) vegetable stock or water
225 g (8 oz) can tomatoes
15 ml (1 tbsp) tomato purée
2.5 ml (½ tsp) chilli powder
salt and pepper
300 ml (½ pint) natural yogurt
4 eggs, hard-boiled

1 Heat the oil in a deep, heavy-based pan. Add the onion, apple and garam masala and fry gently until soft, stirring frequently.

2 Pour in the stock and tomatoes and bring to the boil, stirring to break up the tomatoes as much as possible. Stir in the tomato purée with the chilli powder and salt and pepper to taste. Lower the heat and simmer, uncovered, for 20 minutes to allow the flavours to develop.

3 Cool the sauce slightly, then pour into a blender or food processor. Add half of the yogurt and work to a purée. Return to the rinsed-out pan.

4 Shell the eggs and cut them in half lengthways. Add them to the sauce, cut side up, then simmer very gently for 10 minutes. Taste the sauce and adjust seasoning if necessary. Serve hot, with the remaining yogurt drizzled over the top. Accompany with boiled rice (see page 188) and mango chutney, if liked.

Curried Eggs

PAN-FRIED MINI PIZZAS

MAKES 12

1 quantity of basic pizza dough (see page 184)
30 ml (2 tbsp) olive oil
1 small onion, skinned and finely chopped
1–2 garlic cloves, skinned and crushed
350 g (12 oz) ripe tomatoes, skinned and roughly chopped, or 397 g (14 oz) can tomatoes
20 ml (4 tsp) chopped fresh basil or 10 ml (2 tsp) dried
pinch of raw cane sugar, or to taste
salt and pepper
polyunsaturated oil, for shallow frying

1 Make the basic pizza dough according to the instructions on page 184 and leave to rise.

2 Heat the olive oil in a saucepan, add the onion and garlic and fry gently for 5 minutes until soft and lightly coloured. Add the tomatoes and break them up with a spoon. Bring to the boil, then lower the heat, add the basil, sugar and salt and pepper to taste. Simmer for about 20 minutes, stirring frequently.

3 Meanwhile, turn the risen dough out on to a floured surface, roll out and cut into twelve 10 cm (4 inch) circles.

4 Work the tomato mixture in a blender or food processor. Return to the rinsed-out pan, taste and adjust seasoning, then reheat gently while frying the pizzas.

5 Heat the vegetable oil in a small frying pan and shallow fry the pizzas in batches for about 2 minutes on each side until they are golden.

6 Drain the pizzas quickly on absorbent kitchen paper, then spread with some of the sauce. Serve immediately.

Pan-Fried Mini Pizzas

PANCAKES STUFFED WITH CHEESE AND SPINACH

SERVES 4

450 g (1 lb) washed fresh spinach or 226 g (8 oz) frozen
50 g (2 oz) butter or polyunsaturated margarine
1 small onion, skinned and finely chopped
65 g (2½ oz) freshly grated Parmesan cheese
600 ml (1 pint) béchamel sauce (see page 185)
salt and pepper
100 g (4 oz) plain wholemeal flour
1 egg
300 ml (½ pint) milk
polyunsaturated oil, for frying

1 To make the filling, put the spinach in a saucepan without adding water and cook gently for 5–10 minutes (or until thawed if using frozen spinach). Drain well and chop finely.

2 Melt the butter or margarine in a saucepan, add the onion and fry gently for 5 minutes until soft but not coloured. Stir in the spinach and cook for a further 2 minutes. Remove from the heat and stir in 50 g (2 oz) of the Parmesan cheese, 90 ml (6 tbsp) béchamel sauce and salt and pepper to taste.

3 Make the batter. Put the flour and a pinch of salt in a bowl. Make a well in the centre and add the egg. Beat well with a wooden spoon and gradually beat in the milk.

4 Heat a little oil in an 18 cm (7 inch) heavy-based frying pan until hot, running it round the base and sides of the pan. Pour off any surplus.

5 Pour in just enough batter to coat the base of pan thinly. Fry for 1–2 minutes until golden brown, turn or toss and cook the second side until golden.

6 Transfer the pancake to a plate. Repeat with the remaining batter to make eight pancakes. Pile the cooked pancakes on top of each other with greaseproof paper in between each one.

7 Spread an equal amount of the filling on each pancake, leaving a border around the edge. Roll up and loosely arrange in a single layer in a greased ovenproof dish.

8 Pour over the remaining béchamel sauce and sprinkle with the remaining Parmesan. Bake at 220°C (425°F) mark 7 for about 10 minutes until golden brown. Serve hot.

SPICED RED LENTILS WITH AUBERGINES AND MUSHROOMS

SERVES 6–8

350 g (12 oz) red lentils
5 ml (1 tsp) turmeric
2 garlic cloves, skinned and crushed
1 aubergine
225 g (8 oz) mushrooms, halved
5–10 ml (1–2 tsp) salt
2.5 ml (½ tsp) raw cane sugar
45 ml (3 tbsp) ghee or polyunsaturated oil
5 ml (1 tsp) cumin seeds
5 ml (1 tsp) black mustard seeds
2.5 ml (½ tsp) fennel seeds
5 ml (1 tsp) garam masala
chopped fresh coriander, to garnish

1 Pick over the lentils and remove any grit or discoloured pulses. Put into a sieve and wash thoroughly under cold running water. Drain well.

2 Put the lentils in a large saucepan with the turmeric and garlic. Cover with 1.4 litres (2½ pints) water. Bring to the boil and simmer for about 25 minutes.

3 Meanwhile, wash the aubergine and pat dry with absorbent kitchen paper. Cut into 2.5 cm (1 inch) cubes, discarding the ends.

4 Add the aubergine and mushrooms to the lentils with the salt and sugar. Continue simmering gently for 15–20 minutes, until the vegetables are tender.

5 Heat the ghee or oil in a separate small saucepan, add the remaining spices and fry for 1 minute or until the mustard seeds begin to pop.

6 Stir the spice mixture into the lentils, cover the pan with a tight-fitting lid and remove from the heat. Leave to stand 5 minutes, for the flavours to develop. Turn into a warmed serving dish and garnish with coriander. Serve hot with boiled rice (see page 188), if liked.

Spiced Red Lentils with Aubergines and Mushrooms

OEUFS GRUYÈRE

SERVES 4

40 g (1½ oz) butter or polyunsaturated margarine
100 g (4 oz) button mushrooms, thinly sliced
40 g (1½ oz) plain wholemeal flour
150 ml (¼ pint) milk
150 ml (¼ pint) dry white wine
150 ml (¼ pint) double cream
175 g (6 oz) Gruyère cheese, grated
1.25 ml (¼ tsp) ground mace
salt and pepper
4 eggs, size 2
30 ml (2 tbsp) grated Parmesan cheese
2.5 ml (½ tsp) paprika
about 60 ml (4 tbsp) dried wholemeal breadcrumbs

1 Melt the butter or margarine in a saucepan, add the mushrooms and fry gently for 5 minutes. Remove with a slotted spoon and set aside.

2 Add the flour and cook gently, stirring, for 1–2 minutes. Remove from the heat and gradually blend in the milk and wine. Bring to the boil, stirring constantly, then simmer for 3 minutes until thick and smooth.

3 Lower the heat, stir in the cream, 100g (4 oz) of the Gruyère cheese and cook gently until the cheese melts. Add the mace, salt and pepper and remove from the heat. Stir in the mushrooms.

4 Pour half the sauce into 4 individual gratin dishes. Break an egg in the centre of each dish. Cover with the remaining sauce.

5 Mix the remaining Gruyère with the Parmesan cheese and paprika and sprinkle over the sauce. Cover with the breadcrumbs. Bake at 190°C (375°F) mark 5 for 10–15 minutes. Serve hot.

CABBAGE AND HAZELNUT CROQUETTES

MAKES 16

450 g (1 lb) potatoes, peeled
salt and pepper
900 g (2 lb) cabbage, roughly chopped
45 ml (3 tbsp) milk
50 g (2 oz) butter or polyunsaturated margarine
50 g (2 oz) plain wholemeal flour
50 g (2 oz) hazelnuts, chopped and toasted
2 eggs, beaten
100 g (4 oz) dry wholemeal breadcrumbs
polyunsaturated oil, for deep frying
lemon wedges, to serve

1 Boil the potatoes in salted water for about 20 minutes until tender. Drain them well and mash without adding any liquid.

2 Cook the cabbage in boiling salted water for 5–10 minutes until just tender. Drain well. Purée in a blender or food processor, adding the milk if required – you should have 450 ml (¾ pint) purée.

3 Melt the butter or margarine in a saucepan, add the flour and cook gently, stirring, for 1–2 minutes. Gradually blend in the cabbage purée. Bring to the boil, then simmer for 5 minutes.

4 Stir the mashed potatoes and hazelnuts into the sauce, add salt and pepper to taste and mix well. Transfer to a bowl, cool, cover and chill in the refrigerator for at least 1½ hours or until firm.

5 With dampened hands, shape the mixture into 16 croquettes. Place on a greased baking sheet and chill again for at least 20 minutes.

6 Coat the croquettes in the beaten eggs and breadcrumbs. Heat the oil to 180°C (350°F) in a deep-fat frier. Deep fry the croquettes in batches for about 4 minutes until crisp and golden. Remove with a slotted spoon and drain on absorbent kitchen paper. Serve hot, with lemon wedges.

Cabbage and Hazelnut Croquettes

SPANISH OMELETTE

SERVES 4

45 ml (3 tbsp) olive oil
2 large potatoes, peeled and cut into 1 cm (½ inch) cubes
2 large onions, skinned and coarsely chopped
salt and pepper
6 eggs, lightly beaten

1 In a medium frying pan, gently heat the olive oil. Add the potatoes and onions and season with salt and pepper. Fry, stirring occasionally, for 10–15 minutes until golden brown.

2 Drain off excess oil and quickly stir in the eggs. Cook for 5 minutes, shaking the pan occasionally to prevent sticking. If you wish, place under a hot grill to brown the top. Serve hot.

VARIATIONS

This is a basic Spanish Omelette, but other vegetables may be added, such as chopped red pepper, tomatoes, peas, mushrooms, spinach. Either add them raw at the beginning, or stir cooked vegetables into the eggs (peas and spinach should be added already cooked).

SPINACH ROULADE

SERVES 3–4

900 g (2 lb) spinach, trimmed, or 450 g (1 lb) frozen
4 eggs, size 2, separated
pinch of freshly grated nutmeg
salt and pepper
25 g (1 oz) butter or polyunsaturated margarine
1 medium onion, skinned and finely chopped
100 g (4 oz) curd cheese
50 g (2 oz) Gruyère cheese, grated
30 ml (2 tbsp) soured cream
tomato sauce, to serve (see page 187)

1 Grease a 35.5×25.5 cm (14×10 inch) Swiss roll tin and line with non-stick baking parchment. Set aside. Wash the fresh spinach in several changes of cold water. Place in a saucepan without adding water. Cook gently, covered, for about 5 minutes until wilted or until thawed if using frozen spinach.

2 Drain the spinach well and chop finely. Turn into a bowl and allow to cool slightly for about 5 minutes. Beat in the egg yolks, nutmeg and salt and pepper to taste.

3 Whisk the egg whites until stiff, then fold into the spinach mixture with a large metal spoon until evenly incorporated. Spread the mixture in the prepared tin. Bake at 200°C (400°F) mark 6 for 15–20 minutes until firm.

4 Meanwhile, melt the butter or margarine in a saucepan. Add the onion and fry for about 5 minutes until soft. Remove from the heat and stir in the cheeses, soured cream, and salt and pepper to taste.

5 Turn the roulade out on to greaseproof paper and spread immediately and quickly with the cheese mixture. Roll the roulade up by gently lifting the greaseproof paper. Serve hot cut into thick slices, with the tomato sauce.

Spinach Roulade

SPICY HOT CHICK PEAS STEWED WITH TOMATOES

SERVES 4

225 g (8 oz) dried chick peas, soaked in cold water overnight, or two 425 g (15 oz) cans chick peas, drained
4 garlic cloves, skinned and crushed
60 ml (4 tbsp) ghee or polyunsaturated oil
2 medium onions, skinned and finely chopped
2 small green chillies, seeded and finely chopped
5 ml (1 tsp) turmeric
5 ml (1 tsp) paprika
15 ml (1 tbsp) ground cumin
15 ml (1 tbsp) ground coriander
5 ml (1 tsp) garam masala
4 tomatoes, roughly chopped
30 ml (2 tbsp) chopped fresh coriander
15 ml (1 tbsp) chopped fresh mint
salt and pepper
chopped fresh mint, to garnish

1 Drain the chick peas and place in a large saucepan with half the garlic. Cover with plenty of water, bring to the boil, cover and simmer for 2–3 hours until tender. Drain well and set aside.

2 Heat the ghee or oil in a heavy-based saucepan, add the remaining garlic and the onions and fry gently for about 5 minutes until soft and lightly coloured. Add the chillies, turmeric, paprika, cumin, coriander and garam masala and fry, stirring, for a further 1–2 minutes.

3 Add the tomatoes, coriander and mint and cook, stirring, for 5–10 minutes until the tomatoes turn to a purée.

4 Add the cooked or canned chick peas and stir well. Simmer gently for another 5 minutes, or until the chick peas are heated through. Add salt and pepper to taste, then turn into a warmed serving dish. Serve hot. Accompany with boiled rice (see page 188) and natural yogurt, if liked.

RED KIDNEY BEANS WITH GINGER AND CHILLI

SERVES 4–6

250 g (9 oz) dried red kidney beans, soaked in cold water overnight, or two 425 g (15 oz) cans red kidney beans, drained
2–3 small green chillies
60 ml (4 tbsp) ghee or polyunsaturated oil
2.5 cm (1 inch) piece of fresh root ginger, peeled and finely chopped
2 garlic cloves, skinned and crushed
150 ml (1/4 pint) single cream
60 ml (4 tbsp) tomato purée
salt and pepper
fresh green chilli rings, to garnish

1 Drain the beans and put in a large saucepan. Cover with plenty of water, bring to the boil and boil rapidly for 10 minutes. Simmer for about 40 minutes until tender.

2 Meanwhile, halve and seed the chillies. Chop the flesh finely with a sharp knife. Rinse your hands thoroughly.

3 Heat the ghee or oil in a heavy-based saucepan, add the ginger and garlic and fry gently for 2 minutes. Add the chillies, the cream and tomato purée. Drain the kidney beans thoroughly and add to the pan. Stir well to mix.

4 Cook over gentle heat for 3–4 minutes, or until thoroughly hot, stirring occasionally. Add salt and pepper to taste and turn into a warmed serving dish. Sprinkle with the chilli rings and serve hot with boiled rice (see page 188), if liked.

Red Kidney Beans with Ginger and Chilli

Cheese Stuffed Baked Potatoes

CHEESE STUFFED BAKED POTATOES

Serves 4

4 medium potatoes such as Desirée, King Edward and Maris Piper, about 250 g (8 oz) each
1 medium onion, skinned
25 g (1 oz) butter or polyunsaturated margarine
60 ml (4 tbsp) milk
125 g (4 oz) Cheddar cheese, grated
dash of Worcestershire sauce
salt and pepper
snipped fresh chives, to garnish

1 Scrub the potatoes under cold running water. Pat dry with absorbent kitchen paper and wrap individually in foil. Bake at 200°C (400°F) mark 6 for about 1¼–1½ hours, or until just tender. Remove the potatoes from the oven, leaving the oven turned on.

2 Cut the potatoes in half lengthways. Scoop out most of the flesh, leaving a good rim around the edge. Mash the scooped-out potato in a bowl.

3 Finely chop the onion. Melt the butter or margarine in a saucepan. Add the onion and fry until lightly browned. Add the milk and heat gently.

4 Beat this mixture into the mashed potato with half of the cheese, the Worcestershire sauce and salt and pepper to taste.

5 Spoon back into the shells (or pipe with a large, star nozzle). Sprinkle over the remaining cheese. Return to the oven for about 20 minutes until golden. Serve immediately, sprinkled with chives.

LENTIL CROQUETTES

Makes 8

225 g (8 oz) split red lentils
2 celery sticks, trimmed and finely chopped
1 medium onion, skinned and chopped
1–2 garlic cloves, skinned and crushed
10 ml (2 tsp) garam masala
1 egg, beaten
salt and pepper
30 ml (2 tbsp) wholemeal flour, to coat
5 ml (1 tsp) paprika
5 ml (1 tsp) ground turmeric
60 ml (4 tbsp) polyunsaturated oil
fresh coriander or parsley and lime wedges, to garnish

Lentil Croquettes

1 Put the lentils in a large saucepan with the celery, onion, garlic, 600 ml (1 pint) water and garam masala. Bring to the boil, stirring with a wooden spoon to mix.

2 Lower the heat and simmer gently for 30 minutes or until the lentils are tender and have absorbed all the liquid. Stir frequently to prevent the lentils sticking to the bottom.

3 Remove from the heat. Leave to cool for a few minutes, then beat in the egg and salt and pepper to taste. Turn on to a board or flat plate and spread evenly. Leave until cold, then chill for 30 minutes.

4 With floured hands, form the mixture into 8 triangular croquette shapes. Coat in the flour mixed with the paprika and turmeric. Chill again 30 minutes.

5 Heat the oil in a large frying pan, add the croquettes and fry over moderate–high heat for 10 minutes, turning once, until crisp and golden on both sides. Drain on absorbent kitchen paper and serve hot, with a sprinkling of chopped coriander or parsley on top, and lime wedges. Accompany with yogurt dressing (see page 155), if liked.

CURRIED NUT BURGERS

MAKES 6

90 ml (6 tbsp) polyunsaturated oil
1 medium onion, skinned and finely chopped
15 ml (1 tbsp) Madras curry paste or powder
175 g (6 oz) Edam cheeses, diced
175 g (6 oz) chopped mixed nuts
175 g (6 oz) granary breadcrumbs
2 carrots, peeled and grated
salt and pepper
2 eggs
30 ml (2 tbsp) wholemeal flour, to coat
watercress sprigs, radicchio, cucumber and lemon or lime wedges, to serve

1 Heat 30 ml (2 tbsp) of the oil in a small saucepan, add the onion and curry paste or powder and fry gently for 5 minutes until the onion is soft but not coloured.

2 Put the onion in a bowl with the cheese, 150 g (5 oz) of the nuts and 125 g (4 oz) of the breadcrumbs. Add the carrots and salt and pepper to taste, and stir well to mix. Bind with one of the eggs.

3 With floured hands, form the mixture into 6 burger shapes, coating them lightly with flour. Beat the remaining egg in a shallow dish and dip the burgers in it to coat lightly.

4 Mix the remaining nuts and breadcrumbs together on a flat plate. Coat the burgers in this mixture, pressing on firmly with your hands. Chill the burgers for 30 minutes to firm.

5 Heat the remaining oil in a large frying pan, add the burgers and fry over moderate–high heat for 10 minutes on each side until golden brown and cooked through. Drain on absorbent kitchen paper before serving with the watercress, radicchio and cucumber.

Curried Nut Burgers

FRIED MOZZARELLA SANDWICHES

MAKES 10

175 g (6 oz) Mozzarella cheese
10 large slices wholemeal bread, crusts removed
salt and pepper
2 eggs
175 ml (6 fl oz) milk
75 g (3 oz) plain wholemeal flour
polyunsaturated oil, for frying

1 Slice the cheese thinly and arrange on five slices of bread, leaving a narrow margin around the edges. Season with salt and pepper to taste and cover with the remaining bread slices. Cut each sandwich in half diagonally or widthways.

2 Beat the eggs in a shallow bowl and add the milk. Season with salt and pepper to taste. Spread out the flour on a flat plate. Brush a little egg and milk mixture inside the sandwiches edges and press together.

3 Quickly dip each sandwich into the egg mixture, then coat lightly with flour. Dip again into the egg mixture, shaking off any excess.

4 Pour enough oil into a frying pan to come 1 cm (½ inch) up the sides of the pan and heat until it is hot.

5 Carefully place the sandwiches in the pan, in a single layer. (If your pan is not large enough, use two pans or cook in batches.) Fry for about 3 minutes on each side until brown. Drain on absorbent kitchen paper and serve immediately.

Crunchy Baked Potato Skins

CRUNCHY BAKED POTATO SKINS

SERVES 4

4 medium baking potatoes
60 ml (4 tbsp) polyunsaturated oil
salt and pepper
300 ml (½ pint) natural yogurt
30 ml (2 tbsp) snipped fresh chives

1 Pierce the potatoes all over with a skewer, then place directly on the oven shelf. Bake at 200°C (400°F) mark 6 for 1¼ hours until tender.

2 Cut each potato in half lengthways and scoop out most of the flesh with a sharp-edged teaspoon, taking care not to split the skins.

3 Stand the skins on a lightly oiled baking sheet. Brush inside and out with the oil and sprinkle with salt and pepper to taste. Increase the oven temparature to 220°C (425°F) mark 7 and bake for 10 minutes until crisp.

4 Meanwhile, whisk the yogurt and chives together with salt and pepper to taste. Spoon into a serving bowl or sauceboat. Serve the potato skins piping hot, with the yogurt dressing handed separately.

BARBECUED BEANS

SERVES 4

350 g (12 oz) dried red kidney beans, soaked in cold water overnight
1.1 litres (2 pints) tomato juice
1 large onion, skinned and sliced
30 ml (2 tbsp) soy sauce
60 ml (4 tbsp) cider vinegar
5 ml (1 tsp) vegetable yeast extract
15 ml (1 tbsp) mustard powder
15 ml (1 tbsp) honey
2.5 ml (½ tsp) chilli powder
salt and pepper

1 Drain the beans and place in a saucepan. Cover with cold water, bring to the boil and boil rapidly for 10 minutes, then drain.

2 Put the tomato juice, onion, soy sauce, vinegar, yeast extract, mustard, honey and chilli powder in a flameproof casserole. Bring to the boil and add the beans.

3 Cover and cook in the oven at 140°C (275°F) mark 1 for about 4 hours until the beans are tender. Season with salt and pepper to taste.

GARLIC AND BLACK PEPPERCORN CHEESE

MAKES 450 G (1 LB)

568 ml (1 pint) milk
600 ml (1 pint) single cream
30 ml (2 tbsp) buttermilk
1 garlic clove, skinned
5 ml (1 tsp) salt
15 ml (1 tbsp) chopped fresh mixed herbs (parsley, chervil, chives, thyme)
30 ml (2 tbsp) black peppercorns, coarsely crushed
cucumber slices, to garnish

1 Put the milk and cream in a saucepan and heat gently to blood heat or 32–38°C (90–100°F); stir in the buttermilk. Pour the mixture into a bowl.

2 Cover the bowl with cling film and leave in a warm place for 24–48 hours until the cream mixture turns to soft curds.

3 Line a colander with muslin or all-purpose kitchen cloth and place in the sink. Pour the curds into the colander and drain for 10 minutes.

Garlic and Black Peppercorn Cheese

4 Place the colander on a rack in a saucepan, cover with cling film and chill for 18–24 hours.

5 On a board, crush the garlic to a smooth purée with the flat of a round-bladed knife and the salt. Spoon the curds from the colander into a bowl and stir in the mixed herbs, garlic and peppercorns.

6 Line a small plastic punnet or earthenware cheese mould with a double layer of damp cheesecloth or all-purpose kitchen cloth, leaving a 5 cm (2 inch) overhang. Spoon in the curds and fold the cheesecloth over the top.

7 Invert the punnet or mould on to a wire rack placed over a shallow dish, cover tightly with cling film and chill for 18–24 hours.

8 To serve, unmould the cheese on to a plate, remove the cheesecloth and garnish with cucumber slices. Serve chilled.

POTTED CHEESE WITH MINT

SERVES 6

75 g (3 oz) butter or polyunsaturated margarine, at room temperature
225 g (8 oz) Red Leicester or Cheddar cheese
15 ml (1 tbsp) chopped fresh mint
60 ml (4 tbsp) soured cream
pepper
mint leaves, to garnish
wholemeal bread or crispbreads, to serve

1 Put the butter or margarine in a bowl and beat until really soft. Grate in the cheese, then beat it gradually into the butter or margarine.

2 Stir in the chopped mint and soured cream, adding pepper to taste. (Salt should not be required as the cheese contains sufficient.)

3 Spoon into individual serving dishes and garnish with mint leaves. Cover with cling film and chill for at least 2 hours. To serve, spread on slices of wholemeal bread or crispbreads.

Potted Cheese with Mint

AUBERGINE DIP

SERVES 4

2 large aubergines
3 garlic cloves, skinned
salt
about 150 ml (¼ pint) tahini (paste of finely ground sesame seeds)
juice of about 3 lemons
coriander leaves, black olives and lemon wedges, to garnish
hot wholemeal pitta bread, to serve

1 Place the aubergines under the grill and cook for about 20 minutes, turning constantly until the skin blisters and the flesh feels soft. Remove from the heat and leave until cool enough to handle. Then peel off the skins and discard them.

2 Put the aubergine flesh in a blender or food processor and blend to form smooth purée, or push through a sieve.

3 Crush the garlic with salt then add to the aubergine flesh. Add half the tahini paste and the juice of 1½ lemons and work again until evenly incorporated.

4 Taste the dip and add a little more tahini paste and lemon juice. Continue adding tahini and lemon gradually until the flavour is to your liking. Add more salt if liked.

5 Turn the dip into a shallow serving bowl and smooth the surface. Garnish with coriander, olives and lemon wedges. Refrigerate for 2–3 hours until serving time. Serve with hot pitta bread.

MAIN COURSES

Main courses based on vegetables, pulses, rice, nuts and grains are as nutritious and satisfying as dishes which include meat, poultry or fish. They should be dishes in their own right and provide the important nutrients required for a balanced diet. Some are high in protein and others, such as those based entirely on vegetables, will be low, so accompany these with a dish based on pulses, grains or nuts for a balanced meal. There are a variety of vegetarian dishes in this chapter suitable for both family meals and entertaining.

CAULIFLOWER AND COURGETTE BAKE

SERVES 4

700 g (1½ lb) cauliflower
salt and pepper
50 g (2 oz) butter or polyunsaturated margarine
225 g (8 oz) courgettes, trimmed and thinly sliced
45 ml (3 tbsp) wholemeal flour
150 ml (¼ pint) milk
3 eggs, separated
15 ml (1 tbsp) grated Parmesan cheese

1 Divide the cauliflower into small florets, trimming off thick stalks and leaves. Cook in boiling salted water for 10–12 minutes until tender.

2 Meanwhile, in a separate pan, melt 25 g (1 oz) of the butter or margarine, add the courgettes and cook until beginning to soften. Remove from the pan with a slotted spoon and drain on absorbent kitchen paper.

3 Melt the remaining butter or margarine in the pan, stir in the flour and cook, stirring, for 1–2 minutes. Remove from the heat and add the milk a little at a time, whisking constantly after each addition. Return to the heat and bring to the boil, stirring. Lower the heat and simmer until thickened.

4 Drain the cauliflower well and place in a blender or food processor with the warm sauce, egg yolks and salt and pepper to taste. Blend together until evenly mixed, then turn into a large bowl.

5 Whisk the egg whites until stiff and carefully fold into the cauliflower mixture with a large metal spoon until they are evenly distributed.

6 Spoon half of the mixture into a 1.6 litre (2¾ pint) soufflé dish. Arrange the courgettes on top, reserving a few for garnish, then cover with the remaining cauliflower mixture and reserved drained courgettes.

7 Sprinkle over the Parmesan cheese and bake at 190°C (375°F) mark 5 for 35–40 minutes or until golden. Serve hot.

Cauliflower and Courgette Bake

WHOLEWHEAT MACARONI BAKE

SERVES 4–6

175 g (6 oz) wholewheat macaroni
salt and pepper
30 ml (2 tbsp) polyunsaturated oil
1 medium onion, skinned and chopped
225 g (8 oz) button mushrooms
350 g (12 oz) tomatoes, skinned and roughly chopped
300 ml (½ pint) vegetable stock
15 ml (1 tbsp) tomato purée
5 ml (1 tsp) dried mixed herbs
5 ml (1 tsp) dried oregano
30 ml (2 tbsp) wholemeal flour
300 ml (½ pint) milk
100 g (4 oz) low-fat soft cheese
1 egg, beaten
5 ml (1 tsp) English mustard powder
30 ml (2 tbsp) wholemeal breadcrumbs
30 ml (2 tbsp) grated Parmesan cheese

1 Plunge the macaroni into a large saucepan of boiling salted water. Simmer, uncovered, for 10 minutes.

2 Meanwhile, heat the oil in a separate pan, add the onion and fry gently for 5 minutes until soft.

3 Cut the small mushrooms in half and slice the larger ones. Add to the pan, increase the heat and toss with the onion for 1–2 minutes until the juices run.

4 Add the tomatoes and stock and bring to the boil, stirring constantly to break up the tomatoes. Lower the heat, add the tomato purée, herbs and salt and pepper to taste, and simmer gently for 10 minutes.

5 Drain the macaroni into a colander and leave to stand while making the cheese sauce.

6 Put the flour and milk in a blender or food processor and blend for 1 minute. Transfer to a heavy-based pan and simmer, stirring for 5 minutes until thickened. Remove from the heat and beat in the cheese, egg, mustard and salt and pepper to taste.

7 Mix the macaroni with the mushrooms in tomato sauce, then pour into a baking dish. Pour the cheese sauce over the top and sprinkle with the breadcrumbs and Parmesan.

8 Bake at 190°C (375°F) mark 5 for 20 minutes until golden brown and bubbling. Serve hot, straight from the dish.

Wholewheat Macaroni Bake

MACARONI PIE

SERVES 6

115 g (4½ oz) butter or polyunsaturated margarine
30 ml (2 tbsp) olive oil
1 small onion, skinned and finely chopped
2 garlic cloves, skinned and crushed
397 g (14 oz) can tomatoes
5 ml (1 tsp) chopped fresh basil or 2.5 ml (½ tsp) dried, or mixed herbs
salt and pepper
225 g (8 oz) large wholewheat macaroni
75 g (3 oz) plain wholemeal flour
568 ml (1 pint) milk
75 g (3 oz) Gruyère cheese, grated
1.25 ml (¼ tsp) freshly grated nutmeg
60 ml (4 tbsp) freshly grated Parmesan cheese
45 ml (3 tbsp) dried wholemeal breadcrumbs

1 To make the tomato sauce, melt 50 g (2 oz) of the butter or margarine in a heavy-based saucepan with the olive oil. Add the onion and garlic and fry gently for 5 minutes until soft but not coloured.

2 Add the tomatoes and their juices with the basil and salt and pepper to taste, then stir with a wooden spoon to break up the tomatoes. Bring to the boil, then lower the heat and simmer for 10 minutes, stirring occasionally.

3 Meanwhile, cook the macaroni in a large pan of boiling salted water for 10 minutes or until just tender.

4 For the cheese sauce, melt the remaining butter or margarine in a saucepan, add the flour and cook over low heat, stirring with a wooden spoon, for about 2 minutes. Remove the pan from the heat and gradually blend in the milk, stirring after each addition. Bring to the boil slowly, stirring all the time until the sauce thickens. Add the Gruyère cheese and salt and pepper to taste and stir until melted.

5 Drain the macaroni and mix with the tomato sauce. Arrange half of this mixture in a large greased ovenproof dish.

6 Pour over half of the cheese sauce. Repeat the layers, then sprinkle evenly with the Parmesan cheese and breadcrumbs.

7 Bake the pie at 190°C (375°F) mark 5 for 15 minutes, then brown under a preheated grill for 5 minutes. Serve hot.

SPAGHETTI WITH RATATOUILLE SAUCE

SERVES 4

1 aubergine
salt and pepper
1 medium onion, skinned
1 garlic clove, skinned
1 green pepper
1 red pepper
3 medium courgettes
350 g (12 oz) tomatoes
10 ml (2 tsp) chopped fresh basil
400 g (14 oz) wholewheat spaghetti
freshly grated Parmesan cheese, to serve

1 Dice the aubergine, then spread out on a plate and sprinkle with salt. Leave for 20 minutes to remove bitter flavour.

2 Meanwhile, chop the onion finely. Crush the garlic on a board with a little salt and the flat of the blade of a large knife.

3 Cut the peppers in half and remove the cores and seeds. Slice the flesh into thin strips. Top and tail the courgettes, then slice them into very thin strips.

4 Put the tomatoes in a heatproof bowl and pour in boiling water to cover. Leave to stand for 2 minutes, then drain and plunge into a bowl of cold water. Peel off the skin with your fingers and chop the flesh of the tomatoes finely.

5 Tip the diced aubergine into a sieve and rinse under cold running water. Put into a large, heavy-based pan with the prepared vegetables, basil and salt and pepper to taste. Cover and cook over moderate heat for 30 minutes, shaking the pan and stirring the vegetables frequently to encourage the juices to flow.

6 Meanwhile, cook the spaghetti in a large saucepan of boiling salted water. Simmer, uncovered, for 12 minutes or according to packet instructions, until *al dente* (tender but firm to the bite).

7 Drain the spaghetti thoroughly and turn into a warmed serving dish. Taste and adjust the seasoning of the ratatouille sauce, then pour over the spaghetti. Serve immediately, with the Parmesan cheese handed separately.

Spaghetti with Ratatouille Sauce

WHOLEMEAL VEGETABLE PIE

SERVES 4

3 medium leeks, trimmed
275 g (10 oz) swede, peeled
225 g (8 oz) turnip, peeled
4 medium carrots, peeled
100 g (4 oz) butter or polyunsaturated margarine
225 g (8 oz) large flat mushrooms, sliced
25 g (1 oz) plain wholemeal flour
300 ml (½ pint) vegetable stock
175 g (6 oz) Cheddar cheese, grated
30 ml (2 tbsp) chopped fresh herbs, eg parsley, chives, thyme, marjoram or 10 ml (2 tsp) dried
salt and pepper
175 g (6 oz) wholemeal pastry (see page 183)
beaten egg, to glaze

1 Cut the leek into 2.5 cm (1 inch) lengths, then wash well under cold running water to remove any grit. Cut the swede, turnip and carrots into bite-sized chunks.

2 Melt the butter or margarine in a large saucepan, add the prepared vegetables and fry over moderate heat for about 10 minutes until turning golden brown. Add the mushrooms and cook for a further 2–3 minutes.

3 Sprinkle in the flour and cook gently, stirring, for 1–2 minutes. Gradually blend in the vegetable stock. Bring to the boil, stirring constantly, then simmer for 5–10 minutes or until the vegetables are just tender.

4 Remove the pan from the heat and stir in the cheese, herbs and salt and pepper to taste. Pour into a 1.1 litre (2 pint) pie dish and allow to cool completely for about 1 hour.

5 Roll out the pastry on a floured surface. Cut out a thin strip long enough to go around the rim of the pie dish. Moisten the rim with water and place the strip of pastry on the rim.

6 Roll out the remaining pastry to cover the pie. Moisten the strip of pastry on the rim of the dish, place the lid on top, trim off any excess pastry and press to seal.

7 Knock up and flute or crimp the edge. Decorate the top with any pastry trimmings and brush with beaten egg. Chill in the refrigerator for 15 minutes.

8 Bake the pie at 190°C (375°F) mark 5 for 15–20 minutes until lightly browned. Serve hot.

VEGETABLE LASAGNE

SERVES 4

175 g (6 oz) lasagne verde
salt and pepper
30 ml (2 tbsp) polyunsaturated oil
2 medium onions, skinned and thinly sliced
350 g (12 oz) tomatoes, skinned and thinly sliced
350 g (12 oz) courgettes, trimmed and thinly sliced
15 ml (1 tbsp) tomato purée
5 ml (1 tsp) chopped fresh basil or 2.5 ml (½ tsp) dried
25 g (1 oz) walnut pieces, chopped
450 ml (¾ pint) natural yogurt
2 eggs
75 g (3 oz) Cheddar cheese, grated
1.25 ml (½ tsp) ground cumin
a little polyunsaturated oil, for brushing

1 Cook the lasagne in a large saucepan of boiling salted water with 15 ml (1 tbsp) of the oil for 15 minutes. Drain in single sheets on a clean tea-towel.

2 Heat the remaining oil in a frying pan, add the onion, tomatoes and 300 g (10 oz) of the courgettes and fry gently until the tomatoes begin to break down. Stir in the tomato purée, basil and salt and pepper to taste.

3 Grease a deep-sided 2 litre (3½ pint) ovenproof dish. Layer the vegetables, lasagne and nuts in the dish, ending with a layer of lasagne.

4 Beat the yogurt and eggs together, then stir in the cheese, cumin and salt and pepper to taste. Pour over the lasagne.

5 Arrange the remaining courgettes over the yogurt topping and brush them lightly with oil. Bake the lasagne at 200°C (400°F) mark 6 for about 40 minutes or until set. Serve hot, straight from the dish.

Vegetable Lasagne

THREE BEAN VEGETABLE CURRY

SERVES 6

125 g (4 oz) dried red kidney beans, soaked in cold water overnight
125 g (4 oz) dried soya beans, soaked in cold water overnight
125 g (4 oz) dried black beans, soaked in cold water overnight
700 g (1½ lb) cauliflower
1 medium onion, skinned
½ green pepper, cored and seeded
450 g (1 lb) courgettes, trimmed
1 small piece of fresh root ginger
30 ml (2 tbsp) polyunsaturated oil
125 g (4 oz) button mushrooms
30 ml (2 tbsp) plain wholemeal flour
10 ml (2 tsp) raw cane sugar
20 ml (4 tsp) ground coriander
10 ml (2 tsp) ground cumin
5 ml (1 tsp) turmeric
2.5 ml (½ tsp) chilli powder
15 ml (1 tbsp) tomato purée
900 ml (1½ pints) vegetable stock
salt and pepper

1. Drain the soaked beans and rinse well under cold running water. Put the kidney beans in a large saucepan, cover with plenty of fresh cold water and bring slowly to the boil.

2. Skim off any scum with a slotted spoon, then boil rapidly for 10 minutes. Add the soya beans, half cover the pan with a lid and simmer for 30 minutes. Add the black beans and continue cooking for 1 hour, adding more boiling water as necessary, until tender.

3. Meanwhile, trim the cauliflower and divide into small florets. Slice the onion thinly with the green pepper. Slice the courgettes thickly. Peel the root ginger and crush or chop finely.

4. Heat the oil in a large saucepan, add the onion and pepper and fry gently for 5–10 minutes until lightly browned. Stir in the whole mushrooms and the sliced courgettes and cook for a further 5 minutes.

5. Stir in the ginger, flour, sugar, coriander, cumin, turmeric, chilli powder and tomato purée. Cook, stirring, for 1–2 minutes, then blend in the stock.

6. Drain the beans and add to the pan with the cauliflower. Bring to the boil, add salt and pepper to taste, then lower the heat, cover and simmer for 20 minutes until the vegetables are tender. Serve hot. Accompany with chappatis (see page 160), if liked.

STUFFED AUBERGINES

SERVES 4

4 small aubergines
salt and pepper
30 ml (2 tbsp) olive oil
25 g (1 oz) butter or polyunsaturated margarine
1 small onion, skinned and very finely chopped
4 small ripe tomatoes, skinned and roughly chopped
10 ml (2 tsp) chopped fresh basil or 5 ml (1 tsp) dried
2 eggs, hard-boiled, shelled and roughly chopped
15 ml (1 tbsp) capers
225 g (8 oz) Fontina or Gruyère cheese, sliced

1 Cut the aubergines in half lengthways and scoop out the flesh.

2 Chop the flesh finely, then spread out on a plate and sprinkle with salt. Leave for 20 minutes to remove bitter flavour. Turn aubergine flesh into a colander. Rinse, drain and dry.

3 Heat half of the oil in a frying pan with the butter or margarine, add the onion and fry gently for 5 minutes until soft but not coloured. Add the tomatoes, basil and salt and pepper to taste.

4 Meanwhile, put the aubergines in a single layer in an oiled ovenproof dish. Brush the insides with the remaining oil, then bake at 180°C (350°F) mark 4 for 10 minutes.

5 Spoon half of the tomato mixture into the base of the aubergine shells. Cover with a layer of chopped eggs, capers, then with a layer of cheese. Spoon the remaining tomato mixture over the top. Bake for a further 15 minutes and serve sizzling hot.

MOONG DAL AND SPINACH

SERVES 6

225 g (8 oz) moong dal (split, yellow, washed moong beans)
900 g (2 lb) fresh spinach, washed and trimmed, or 450 g (1 lb) chopped frozen spinach
75 ml (3 fl oz) ghee or polyunsaturated oil
1 medium onion, skinned and finely chopped
15 g (½ oz) fresh root ginger, peeled and finely chopped
1 garlic clove, skinned and crushed
10 ml (2 tsp) ground coriander
5 ml (1 tsp) turmeric
2.5 ml (½ tsp) chilli powder
salt and pepper
lemon wedges, to garnish

1 Rinse the dal under cold running water. Put in a bowl, cover with cold water and leave to soak for about 2 hours. Drain.

2 Place the fresh spinach in a saucepan with only the water that clings to the leaves. Cover and cook for about 5 minutes until tender. Drain well and chop roughly. If using frozen spinach, put in a pan and cook for 7–10 minutes to remove as much liquid as possible.

3 Heat the ghee in a large frying pan, add the onion, ginger and garlic and fry gently for 2–3 minutes until lightly coloured.

4 Stir in the coriander, turmeric, chilli powder and the dal. Fry, stirring, for 2–3 minutes.

5 Pour in 300 ml (½ pint) water, add salt and pepper to taste and bring to the boil. Cover and simmer for about 15 minutes or until the dal is almost tender. Add a little more water if necessary, but the mixture should be almost dry.

6 Stir in the spinach and cook, stirring, for 2–3 minutes until heated through. Taste and adjust the seasoning and serve garnished with lemon wedges. Accompany with chappatis (see page 160), if liked.

Stuffed Aubergines

Moong Dal and Spinach

BUCKWHEAT AND LENTIL CASSEROLE

Serves 4

150 g (5 oz) buckwheat
salt and pepper
30 ml (2 tbsp) polyunsaturated oil
1 red or green pepper, cored, seeded and cut into strips
1 medium onion, skinned and finely chopped
350 g (12 oz) courgettes, trimmed and sliced
175 g (6 oz) mushrooms, sliced
225 g (8 oz) red lentils
3 bay leaves
30 ml (2 tbsp) lemon juice
1 garlic clove, skinned and crushed
2 rosemary sprigs
5 ml (1 tsp) cumin seeds
600 ml (1 pint) vegetable stock
25 g (1 oz) butter or polyunsaturated margarine
chopped fresh parsley, to garnish

Buckwheat and Lentil Casserole

1. Bring 450 ml (¾ pint) water to the boil in a saucepan, sprinkle in the buckwheat, add a pinch of salt and return to the boil. Boil rapidly for 1 minute. Reduce the heat, cover and cook gently, without stirring, for 12 minutes or until the water has been absorbed. Transfer to a greased casserole.

2. Heat the oil in a flameproof casserole and fry the pepper and onion for 5 minutes. Add the courgettes and mushrooms and fry for 5 minutes. Stir in the lentils, bay leaves, lemon juice, garlic, rosemary, cumin and stock. Add to the casserole and stir well.

3. Simmer for 45 minutes until lentils are cooked, stirring occasionally. Add the butter or margarine, adjust the seasoning and sprinkle with parsley. Serve with boiled rice (see page 188) and grated cheese, if liked.

ONION SOUFFLÉ QUICHE

Serves 2–4

175 g (6 oz) wholemeal pastry (see page 183)
2 medium onions, skinned and thinly sliced
300 ml (½ pint) milk
1 bay leaf
1 clove
25 g (1 oz) butter or polyunsaturated margarine
25 g (1 oz) plain wholemeal flour
2 eggs, separated
salt and pepper

1. Roll out the pastry and use to line a 20.5 cm (8 inch) quiche tin or flan dish. Prick the base with a fork, then line with foil and baking beans. Bake at 200°C (400°F) mark 6 for 15 minutes. Remove the foil and beans and bake for a further 5 minutes.

2. Put the onions in a pan with the milk, bay leaf and clove. Cover and simmer for 25 minutes until the onion is tender. Discard the bay leaf and clove.

3. Melt the butter or margarine in a saucepan, add the flour and cook gently, stirring, for 1–2 minutes. Remove from the heat and gradually blend in the onion and milk mixture. Bring to the boil, stirring constantly, then simmer for 3 minutes until thick and smooth. Remove from the heat and beat in the egg yolks with salt and pepper to taste.

4. Whisk the egg whites until stiff but not dry. Gently fold into the onion mixture and spoon into the pastry case. Bake at 220°C (425°F) mark 7 for 30–35 minutes or until just set. Serve immediately.

VEGETABLE HOT POT

Serves 4

450 g (1 lb) carrots, peeled and thinly sliced
2 large onions, skinned and thinly sliced
3 celery sticks, trimmed and thinly sliced
450 g (1 lb) potatoes, peeled and sliced
100 g (4 oz) swede, peeled and thinly sliced
450 ml (¾ pint) vegetable stock
bouquet garni
salt and pepper
425 g (15 oz) can butter beans, drained
100 g (4 oz) frozen peas
175 g (6 oz) fresh wholemeal breadcrumbs
175 g (6 oz) Cheddar cheese, grated

1. Layer the carrot, onion, celery, potato and swede in a 2.3 litre (4 pint) casserole. Pour in the stock and add bouquet garni and salt and pepper to taste.

2. Cover and cook the vegetables at 180°C (350°F) mark 4 for 1 hour. Take the casserole out but leave the oven on at the same setting.

3. Remove the bouquet garni and add the beans and peas. Mix the breadcrumbs and cheese together and spoon over the hot pot. Return to the oven, uncovered, for 20 minutes. Serve immediately.

VEGETABLE COUSCOUS

Serves 6

450 g (1 lb) couscous
4 courgettes, trimmed and cut into 1 cm (½ inch) slices
1 red pepper, cored, seeded and diced
1 green pepper, cored, seeded and diced
2 medium onions, skinned and diced
2 carrots, peeled and diced
225 g (8 oz) turnips, peeled and diced
1 small cauliflower, cut into small florets
4 large tomatoes, skinned and chopped
2 garlic cloves, skinned and crushed
1.1 litres (2 pints) vegetable stock
salt and pepper
225 g (8 oz) chick peas, soaked in cold water overnight, then drained
25 g (1 oz) blanched almonds
5 ml (1 tsp) ground turmeric
10 ml (2 tsp) paprika
2.5 ml (½ tsp) ground coriander
75 g (3 oz) butter or polyunsaturated margarine
100 g (4 oz) dried apricots, soaked overnight

Vegetable Couscous

1. Put the couscous in a large bowl with 450 ml (¾ pint) tepid water and leave to soak for 1 hour.

2. Place the prepared vegetables in a large saucepan with the garlic, stock, pepper to taste, chick peas, almonds and spices. Bring to the boil, cover and simmer for 30 minutes.

3. Drain the couscous and put in a steamer over the saucepan of vegetables. Cover and continue cooking for a further 40 minutes, then remove steamer and cover saucepan.

4. Place the couscous in a large mixing bowl. Beat the butter or margarine into the couscous with 50 ml (2 fl oz) lightly salted water. Leave 15 minutes.

5. Drain and quarter the apricots, add them to the vegetables and simmer for 15 minutes. Stir the couscous to remove lumps and return to the steamer over the simmering vegetables for 20 minutes, covered.

6. Season the vegetables and serve them with the couscous on a warmed serving dish.

PIZZA WITH FOUR CHEESES

Makes 4

1 quantity of basic pizza dough (see page 184)
226 g (8 oz) can tomatoes
salt and pepper
100 g (4 oz) Mozzarella cheese, diced
100 g (4 oz) Bel Paese or Provolone cheese, diced
100 g (4 oz) Fontina or Gruyère cheese, diced
100 g (4 oz) Taleggio cheese, diced
20 ml (4 tsp) olive oil
20 ml (4 tsp) chopped fresh mixed herbs or 10 ml (2 tsp) dried

1 Make the basic pizza dough as on page 184 and leave to rise. Then turn out on to a floured surface, roll out and cut into four 20 cm (8 inch) circles, using sandwich tins or flan rings as a guide. Make the edges slightly thicker than the centres.

2 Put the dough into oiled sandwich tins or flan rings placed on oiled baking sheets. Crush the tomatoes with their juice and spread evenly over the dough, right to the edges. Season with salt and pepper to taste.

3 Mix the four cheeses together and sprinkle them evenly over the four pizzas. Sprinkle over the oil and herbs, with salt and pepper to taste.

4 Leave the pizzas to prove in a warm place for about 30 minutes, then bake at 220°C (425°F) mark 7 for 25 minutes or until the cheeses are melted and the dough is well risen. Swap over on the oven shelves halfway through the cooking time. Serve hot or cold.

LEEK TART

Serves 6

75 ml (5 tbsp) polyunsaturated oil
225 g (8 oz) plain wholemeal flour, plus 30 ml (2 tbsp)
salt and pepper
75 g (3 oz) butter or polyunsaturated margarine
1.4 kg (3 lb) leeks, white parts only, sliced – 700 g (1½ lb) prepared weight
450 ml (¾ pint) milk
pinch of freshly grated nutmeg
2 eggs
75 g (3 oz) Gruyère cheese, grated

1 To make the pastry, put the oil and 30 ml (2 tbsp) cold water in a bowl. Beat well with a fork to form an emulsion. Mix the 225 g (8 oz) flour and a pinch of salt together. Gradually add to the oil mixture to make a dough.

2 Roll out the dough on a floured surface or between pieces of greaseproof paper, and use to line a 25 cm (10 inch) flan tin or dish. Prick the base, line with foil or greaseproof paper and baking beans and bake at 190°C (375°F) mark 5 for 10 minutes until set.

3 Meanwhile, melt 50 g (2 oz) of the butter or margarine in a heavy saucepan. Add the leeks, cover and stew very gently, without allowing to colour, for 10 minutes. Add just enough water to stop the leeks from burning, shake the pan and cook until tender.

4 In a saucepan, melt the remaining butter or margarine, stir in the 30 ml (2 tbsp) flour and cook for 1–2 minutes without allowing to brown. Gradually stir in the milk and cooking liquid from the leeks until smooth. Add the nutmeg and salt and pepper to taste and simmer for a few minutes, stirring continuously.

5 Spread the leeks out evenly in the pastry case. Beat the eggs and add to the white sauce with half the grated cheese. Pour over leeks and sprinkle with the remaining cheese. Bake at 200°C (400°F) mark 6 for 25–30 minutes or until the top is slightly risen and golden brown.

Leek Tart

COURGETTE QUICHE

SERVES 4

175 g (6 oz) plain wholemeal flour
salt and pepper
125 g (4 oz) butter or polyunsaturated margarine
125 g (4 oz) Cheddar cheese, grated
4 eggs
350 g (12 oz) courgettes
150 ml (¼ pint) double cream
10 ml (2 tsp) chopped fresh basil
finely grated rind of 1 lime (optional)

1 To make the pastry, put the flour into a bowl with a pinch of salt. Add the butter or margarine in pieces and rub in thoroughly with the fingertips until the mixture resembles fine breadcrumbs.

2 Stir in the cheese. Separate 1 egg, reserve the egg white and add the yolk to the mixture. Gather the mixture together with your fingers to make a smooth ball of dough. Wrap and chill the dough for about 30 minutes.

3 Meanwhile, trim the ends off the courgettes and cut into 2 cm (¾ inch) chunks. Plunge into boiling salted water, bring back to the boil, then simmer for 3 minutes. Drain and set aside.

4 Put the remaining 3 eggs in a jug and beat lightly together with the cream. Stir in the basil, lime rind if using, and salt and pepper to taste. Set aside.

5 Roll out the chilled dough on a floured surface and use to line a loose-bottomed 23 cm (9 inch) flan tin. Refrigerate for 15 minutes.

6 Prick the base of the dough with a fork, then line with foil and baking beans. Stand the tin on a preheated baking sheet and bake at 200°C (400°F) mark 6 for 10 minutes.

7 Remove the foil and beans and brush the inside of the pastry case with a little of the reserved egg white to seal. Return to the oven for 5 minutes.

8 Stand the courgette chunks upright in pastry case; slowly pour in the egg and cream mixture and bake for a further 20 minutes. Serve warm.

CHEESE AND NUT ROAST WITH HOT TOMATO SAUCE

SERVES 4–6

25 g (1 oz) butter or polyunsaturated margarine
1 medium onion, skinned and finely chopped
125 g (4 oz) Sage Derby cheese or Cheddar cheese plus 5 ml (1 tsp) dried sage (optional)
50 g (2 oz) hazelnuts, finely chopped
50 g (2 oz) Brazil nuts, finely chopped
125 g (4 oz) unsalted peanuts, finely chopped
125 g (4 oz) fresh wholemeal breadcrumbs
2 eggs
salt and pepper
600 ml (1 pint) tomato sauce (see page 187)

1 Grease and base-line a 900 ml (1½ pint) loaf tin. Melt the butter or margarine in a saucepan, add the onion and fry gently for about 5 minutes or until soft and just beginning to brown. Transfer to a bowl and finely grate the cheese into the bowl.

2 Stir to mix with the onion, adding the sage if using. Add the nuts, breadcrumbs, and eggs, mixing well and seasoning to taste with salt and pepper. Press the mixture evenly into the tin and bake at 180°C (350°F) mark 4 for about 45 minutes until golden brown.

3 Leave the nut roast to cool in the tin for 2–3 minutes, then turn out on to a warmed serving dish. Cut into slices and serve hot with tomato sauce.

Cheese and Nut Roast with Hot Tomato Sauce

MIXED VEGETABLE KORMA

SERVES 4

50 ml (2 fl oz) ghee or polyunsaturated oil
1 large onion, skinned and finely chopped
3 green chillies, seeded and finely chopped
5 ml (1 tsp) chilli powder
1.25 ml (1/4 tsp) turmeric
60 ml (4 tbsp) tomato purée
300 ml (1/2 pint) natural yogurt
225 g (8 oz) young turnips, peeled and sliced
225 g (8 oz) small carrots, peeled and diced
225 g (8 oz) cauliflower florets
225 g (8 oz) frozen peas
450 ml (3/4 pint) thin coconut milk (see page 187)
salt
8 whole green cardamoms
8 whole cloves
8 black peppercorns
10 ml (2 tsp) fennel seeds
1.25 ml (1/4 tsp) freshly grated nutmeg

1 Heat the ghee or oil in a heavy-based saucepan or flameproof casserole, add the onion and fry gently for about 5 minutes until soft and lightly coloured. Add the chillies and stir to mix. Add the chilli powder and turmeric and fry, stirring, for 2 minutes.

2 Add the tomato purée and stir for a further 2 minutes, then add the yogurt 15 ml (1 tbsp) at a time. Cook each addition over high heat, stirring constantly, until thc yogurt is absorbed.

3 Add the turnips and carrots and fry, stirring frequently, for 5 minutes. Then put in the cauliflower and peas and fry for 5 minutes more.

4 Gradually pour in the coconut milk, stirring all the time. Add salt to taste and bring to the boil. Lower the heat and simmer, uncovered, for about 20 minutes until the vegetables are tender and the sauce is absorbed.

5 Meanwhile, split each cardamom and remove the seeds. Dry-fry the whole spices for a few minutes, then crush to a fine powder with a pestle and mortar. Sprinkle the spices over the vegetables and fold gently to mix.

6 Cover the pan with a tight-fitting lid and remove from the heat. Leave to stand for 5 minutes, for the flavours to develop. Taste and adjust seasoning, turn into a warmed serving dish and serve hot. Accompany with chana dal (see page 135) or dry moong dal (see page 132), chappatis (see page 160) and natural yogurt, if liked.

Mixed Vegetable Korma

BROWN RICE RING AND EGGS

SERVES 4

225 g (8 oz) long grain brown rice
salt and pepper
30 ml (2 tbsp) polyunsaturated oil
juice of 1 lemon
45 ml (3 tbsp) wholegrain mustard
2 celery sticks, trimmed and finely chopped
225 g (8 oz) button mushrooms, finely sliced
100 g (4 oz) hazelnuts, roughly chopped
30 ml (2 tbsp) chopped mixed fresh herbs (parsley, marjoram, mint, basil, coriander)
6 eggs, hard-boiled
175 g (6 oz) low-fat soft cheese
watercress sprigs or orange and lemon slices, to garnish

1. Cook the rice in a large saucepan of boiling salted water for about 30 minutes (or according to packet instructions) until tender. Drain thoroughly.

2. Tip the hot rice into a bowl. Mix together the oil, lemon juice, 30 ml (2 tbsp) of the mustard and fork through the rice. Add celery, mushrooms, nuts, herbs, salt and pepper to taste and fork through again.

3. Spoon into a lightly oiled 750 ml (1¼ pint) ring mould, pressing down firmly so that the ingredients cling together. Chill for at least 1 hour.

4. Meanwhile, cut the hard-boiled eggs in half lengthways and scoop out the yolks into a bowl. Add the cheese, remaining mustard and salt and pepper to taste and mash well together. Pipe or spoon the mixture back into the egg cavities.

5. To serve, place a serving plate on top of the ring mould and invert them to turn out the rice ring. Fill the centre with watercress. Serve at room temperature with the eggs.

CREAMY WATERCRESS QUICHE

SERVES 4

175 g (6 oz) wholemeal pastry (see page 183)
50 g (2 oz) butter or polyunsaturated margarine
1 large onion, skinned and chopped
1 bunch watercress, chopped
2 eggs
150 ml (¼ pint) milk
150 ml (¼ pint) single cream
salt and pepper

1. Line a 20.5 cm (8 inch) flan dish with the pastry. Place the dish on a baking sheet then line with foil and baking beans. Bake blind at 200°C (400°F) mark 6 for 10–15 minutes until set but not browned.

2. Melt the butter or margarine in a saucepan, add the onion and cook, stirring occasionally, for 3 minutes until soft. Add the watercress, reserving a sprig to garnish, and cook for a further 3–4 minutes. Remove the pan from the heat and set aside.

3. Whisk together the eggs, milk, cream and salt and pepper to taste. Stir in the cooked watercress mixture and pour into the flan case. Bake at 190°C (375°F) mark 5 for 35 minutes or until set. Serve hot or warm, garnished with a sprig of watercress.

LENTIL AND CELERY PEPPERS

SERVES 2

125 g (4 oz) red lentils
salt and pepper
2 green peppers, about 175 g (6 oz) each
25 g (1 oz) butter or polyunsaturated margarine
1 medium onion, skinned and finely chopped
75 g (3 oz) celery, trimmed and finely chopped
75 g (3 oz) low-fat soft cheese
1 egg

1. Cook the lentils in boiling salted water for 12–15 minutes until just tender. Drain well. Preheat the grill to moderate.

2. Meanwhile, halve the peppers and remove the cores and seeds. Place on a steamer and steam, covered, for about 15 minutes or until soft. Remove from the steamer and leave to cool.

3. Melt the butter or margarine in a frying pan, add the onion and celery and fry gently for 2–3 minutes. Add the lentils to the pan and cook, stirring, for 1–2 minutes until heated through.

4. Remove the pan from the heat and beat in the cheese and egg with salt and pepper to taste.

5. Spoon a little of the mixture into each pepper half. Put the filled peppers under the grill for about 5 minutes or until golden brown. Serve hot with warm wholemeal bread, if liked.

SORREL SOUFFLÉ

SERVES 4

100 g (4 oz) sorrel
50 g (2 oz) butter or polyunsaturated margarine
225 g (8 oz) button mushrooms, finely chopped
1 garlic clove, skinned and crushed
45 ml (3 tbsp) plain wholemeal flour
200 ml (7 fl oz) milk
salt and pepper
225 g (8 oz) Fontina or Gruyère cheese, grated
3 eggs, separated

1 Trim any tough stalks off the sorrel and discard. Wash and drain the leaves and chop them finely.

2 Melt the butter or margarine in a large saucepan, add the sorrel, mushrooms and garlic. Stir over a high heat for 1–2 minutes, then stir in the flour and cook for a further 1 minute.

3 Remove from the heat and gradually stir in the milk and salt and pepper to taste. Bring to the boil, stirring, then cook for 1 minute. Remove from the heat and beat in 200 g (7 oz) of the cheese followed by the egg yolks.

4 Whisk the egg whites until stiff but not dry. Fold lightly into the sauce mixture. Spoon into a 1.4 litre (2½ pint) greased soufflé dish and sprinkle over remaining grated cheese evenly.

5 Bake at 190°C (375°F) mark 5 for about 40 minutes or until well risen, browned and just set. Serve at once, piping hot.

NOTE

The herb sorrel looks like spinach, but it has a rather stronger, more bitter flavour which is nevertheless delicious when used in small quantities, as here. Sorrel is not always easy to obtain in shops, but it is easy to grow in a sunny spot in the garden. If you find sorrel difficult to obtain, you can of course make the soufflé with spinach instead.

AUBERGINE GALETTE

SERVES 4

1.4 kg (3 lb) aubergines
salt and pepper
900 g (2 lb) fresh tomatoes, skinned and quartered, or two 397 g (14 oz) cans tomatoes, drained
30 ml (2 tbsp) tomato purée
1 garlic clove, skinned and crushed
50 ml (2 fl oz) olive oil, plus oil for frying and drizzling over cheese
5 ml (1 tsp) raw cane sugar
15 ml (1 tbsp) chopped fresh basil or 5 ml (1 tsp) dried
200 g (7 oz) Mozzarella cheese, thinly sliced
50 g (2 oz) grated Parmesan cheese
fresh basil sprig, to garnish

1 Slice the aubergines into 0.5 cm (¼ inch) slices and place in a colander or large sieve. Sprinkle with salt and set aside for 30 minutes to remove bitter flavour.

2 Meanwhile, make the tomato sauce. Put the tomatoes, tomato purée, garlic, olive oil, sugar and basil in a saucepan. Stir well and simmer gently for 20 minutes until the liquid is reduced by half. Season with salt and pepper to taste.

3 Rinse the aubergine slices thoroughly under cold running water, drain, then pat dry with absorbent kitchen paper. Heat a little olive oil in a frying pan and fry, a few at a time, adding more oil as required, until golden brown on both sides. Drain on absorbent kitchen paper.

4 Layer the aubergine slices, tomato sauce, Mozzarella cheese and half the Parmesan cheese in a greased shallow ovenproof dish, finishing with a layer of aubergine. Scatter over the remaining Parmesan and drizzle over some olive oil.

5 Bake at 180°C (350°F) mark 4 for 50–60 minutes until the cheese is golden and the sides bubbling. Garnish with a sprig of basil.

Aubergine Galette

SPICED PEPPER AND ONION FLAN

SERVES 4

175 g (6 oz) wholemeal pastry (see page 183)
15 ml (1 tbsp) polyunsaturated oil
2 medium onions, skinned and thinly sliced
1 red pepper, seeded and sliced
25 g (1 oz) butter or polyunsaturated margarine
30 ml (2 tbsp) plain wholemeal flour
5 ml (1 tsp) ground cumin
150 ml (¼ pint) milk
150 ml (¼ pint) natural yogurt
2 egg yolks
30 ml (2 tbsp) grated Parmesan cheese

1 Roll out the pastry on a lightly floured surface and use to line a 20.5 cm (8 inch) plain flan ring placed on a baking sheet. Chill for 15–20 minutes, then line with foil and baking beans. Bake at 200°C (400°F) mark 6 for 10–15 minutes until set but not browned.

2 Heat the oil in a frying pan. Fry the onion and pepper, reserving a few slices to garnish, in the hot oil for 4–5 minutes. Spread over the base of the flan case.

3 Melt the butter or margarine and stir in the flour and cumin. Cook for 2 minutes before adding the milk and yogurt. Bring to the boil, stirring briskly and simmer for 2–3 minutes. Beat in the egg yolks.

4 Pour over the onion and pepper and sprinkle with the Parmesan cheese. Bake at 190°C (375°F) mark 5 for 35–40 minutes. Serve hot garnished with pepper slices.

SALSIFY AU GRATIN

SERVES 4

450 g (1 lb) salsify, trimmed and peeled
300 ml (½ pint) vegetable stock
25 g (1 oz) butter or polyunsaturated margarine
45 ml (3 tbsp) plain wholemeal flour
2.5 ml (½ tsp) mustard powder
175 g (6 oz) mature Cheddar cheese, grated
salt and pepper
50 g (2 oz) fresh wholemeal breadcrumbs

1 Cut the salsify into 2.5 cm (1 inch) lengths and put in a saucepan with the stock. Bring to the boil, cover and simmer gently for 15–20 minutes until tender. Drain, reserving the stock, and put the salsify into an ovenproof dish.

2 Melt the butter or margarine in a saucepan, add the flour and mustard powder and cook over low heat, stirring with a wooden spoon, for 2 minutes. Remove the pan from the heat and gradually blend in the reserved stock, stirring after each addition to prevent lumps forming.

3 Bring to the boil slowly, then simmer for 2–3 minutes, stirring. Add half the cheese and salt and pepper to taste and pour over the salsify.

4 Mix the remaining cheese with the breadcrumbs and sprinkle over the dish. Bake at 190°C (375°F) mark 5 for 20–25 minutes until the top is golden brown. Serve hot.

SPINACH TIMBALE

SERVES 4

25 g (1 oz) butter or polyunsaturated margarine
1 medium onion, skinned and finely chopped
900 g (2 lb) fresh spinach, washed, trimmed and roughly chopped
150 ml (¼ pint) milk
150 ml (¼ pint) single cream
4 eggs
50 g (2 oz) Gruyère cheese, grated
50 g (2 oz) fresh wholemeal breadcrumbs
pinch of freshly grated nutmeg
salt and pepper
thin tomato strips and fresh coriander, to garnish
tomato sauce (see page 187)

1 Melt the butter or margarine in a saucepan, stir in the onion and cook gently for about 5 minutes until soft. Stir in the spinach and cook for a further 5 minutes until soft, stirring occasionally. Stir in the milk and cream and heat gently.

2 Beat the eggs in a large bowl and stir in the spinach mixture, cheese, breadcrumbs, nutmeg and salt and pepper to taste.

3 Turn the mixture into a greased 1.1 litre (2 pint) ring mould, cover with foil and place in a roasting tin half filled with hot water. Bake at 180°C (350°F) mark 4 for 1¼ hours until firm to the touch and a knife, inserted in the centre, comes out clean. Meanwhile, prepare the tomato sauce as on page 187.

4 Remove the ring mould from the water and leave for 5 minutes. Loosen the timbale from the sides of the mould with a knife and turn out on to a warmed flat serving dish. Garnish with thin tomato strips and coriander and serve with the tomato sauce.

LEEK AND CHEESE PIE

SERVES 4

3 large leeks, total weight about 450 g (1 lb), trimmed
6 spring onions
40 g (1½ oz) butter or polyunsaturated margarine
1 egg and 1 egg yolk
30 ml (2 tbsp) double cream
175 g (6 oz) Gruyère cheese, grated
pinch of cayenne
freshly grated nutmeg
salt and pepper
225 g (8 oz) wholemeal pastry (see page 183)

1 Cut the leeks into 1 cm (½ inch) slices, then rinse well under cold running water to remove any grit. Trim the spring onions and chop finely.

2 Melt the butter or margarine in a large frying pan and, when foaming, add the leeks. Cook over moderate heat for 5–7 minutes, stirring occasionally, then add the spring onions. Cook for a further 2 minutes or until the leeks and spring onions are soft but not coloured. Remove from the heat and allow to cool for 5 minutes.

3 Mix the egg, egg yolk, cream and Gruyère cheese in a bowl. Stir in the leek mixture and add the cayenne with the nutmeg and salt and pepper to taste.

4 Cut the pastry into 2 pieces, 1 slightly larger than the other. Shape the larger piece into a ball and roll out until 3 mm (⅛ inch) thick and 2.5 cm (1 inch) larger than the top of a 20.5 cm (8 inch) pie dish.

5 Lift the pastry on to the pie dish taking care not to stretch it. Ease it into place by pressing with your fingertips, working outwards from the centre and up the sides. Spoon the leek and cheese filling into the lined dish, mounding it up slightly in the centre.

6 Roll out the remaining pastry for the lid until it is 1 cm (½ inch) larger than the circumference of the dish. Moisten the pastry round the rim of the dish, place the lid on top, trim off any excess pastry and press to seal.

7 Knock up and flute or crimp the edges. Decorate the top with any pastry trimmings and brush with the beaten egg. Make a slash in the centre of the pie to allow steam to escape.

8 Bake at 200°C (400°F) mark 6 for about 30 minutes or until lightly brown. Allow to cool for about 30 minutes before serving. Serve warm or cold.

VEGETABLE KEBABS WITH TOFU SAUCE

SERVES 2

297 g (10½ oz) silken tofu
30 ml (2 tbsp) olive oil
20 ml (4 tsp) soy sauce
about 30 ml (2 tbsp) lemon juice
1–2 garlic cloves, skinned and crushed
15 ml (1 tbsp) sesame oil (optional)
salt and pepper
4 small courgettes, trimmed
6 pieces baby sweetcorn, halved crossways
16 button mushrooms
12 cherry tomatoes or 3 medium tomatoes, quartered
12 bay leaves
30 ml (2 tbsp) sesame seeds

1. Put the tofu in a blender or food processor with half the oil and soy sauce, the lemon juice, garlic and sesame oil (if using). Work until evenly combined, then add salt and pepper to taste and more lemon juice, if liked. Pour into a jug and chill.

2. Cut each courgette into 3. Blanch in boiling salted water for 1 minute, then drain. Thread vegetables and bay leaves on to oiled skewers.

3. Mix the remaining oil and soy sauce with the sesame seeds. Brush over the kebabs. Cook under a preheated grill for about 10 minutes, turning and brushing frequently. Serve hot, on a bed of boiled rice (see page 188), if liked, with the tofu sauce handed separately.

NOTE

Tofu is also known as soya bean curd. It is off-white in colour and is formed into soft blocks. Tofu can be bought by weight from Chinese stores or in cartons from health food shops. Of the three forms, silken tofu is the softest and ideal for sauces. Firm tofu is made from heavily pressed bean curd and soft tofu has a texture between the two. Tofu is high in protein, fairly low in carbohydrate and fat and is a good source of calcium, iron and the B vitamins, thiamin and riboflavin.

Vegetable Kebabs with Tofu Sauce

CELERIAC AU GRATIN

SERVES 4

15 ml (1 tbsp) lemon juice
2 heads celeriac, total weight about 900 g (2 lb)
salt and pepper
100 g (4 oz) butter or polyunsaturated margarine
150 ml (¼ pint) dry white wine
175 g (6 oz) Gruyère cheese, grated
75 g (3 oz) Parmesan cheese, freshly grated

1 Fill a bowl with cold water and add the lemon juice. Peel the celeriac, then cut into chunky pieces, putting them into the acidulated water to prevent discoloration.

2 Drain the celeriac, then plunge quickly into a large pan of boiling salted water. Return to the boil and blanch for 10 minutes. Drain thoroughly.

3 Melt the butter or margarine in a flameproof gratin dish. Add the celeriac and turn to coat in the butter or margarine. Stir in the wine. Mix together the Gruyère and Parmesan cheeses and sprinkle over the top of the celeriac, with salt and pepper to taste. Bake at 190°C (375°F) mark 5 for 30 minutes until the celeriac is tender when pierced with a skewer and the topping is golden brown.

Celeriac Au Gratin

MIXED VEGETABLE CURRY

SERVES 3–4

900 g (2 lb) mixed vegetables (eg potatoes, cauliflower, okra, carrots, beans, peas)
60 ml (4 tbsp) polyunsaturated oil
15 ml (1 tbsp) mustard seeds
5 ml (1 tsp) ground cumin
2.5 ml (½ tsp) ground fenugreek
2 medium onions, skinned and sliced
2.5 ml (½ tsp) turmeric
salt
2 tomatoes, skinned and chopped
juice of ½ lemon

1 Blanch the vegetables in boiling water. (Potatoes for 10 minutes; cauliflower, okra and carrots for 3 minutes; beans and peas for 2 minutes.) Drain and set aside.

2 Heat the oil in a flameproof casserole and add the mustard seeds, cumin and fenugreek. Cover the casserole and fry gently for 2–3 minutes, shaking the casserole constantly so that the spices do not scorch.

3 Add the onions and turmeric to the spices and fry gently for 5 minutes until the onions soften.

4 Add the vegetables to the pan with salt to taste and moisten with a few spoonfuls of water. Cover the casserole and cook gently for about 5 minutes, stirring occasionally, until the vegetables are tender but still crisp.

5 Add the tomatoes and lemon juice and taste and adjust seasoning. Cook for 1 minute more and then turn into a warmed serving dish. Serve hot with boiled rice (see page 188) and a bowl of yogurt and grated cucumber, if liked.

Mixed Vegetable Curry

STUFFED PEPPERS

SERVES 6

3 green peppers
3 red peppers
50 g (2 oz) butter or polyunsaturatred margarine
1 onion, skinned and finely chopped
100 g (4 oz) long grain brown rice
450 ml (¾ pint) vegetable stock
15 ml (1 tbsp) tomato purée
100 g (4 oz) mushrooms, sliced
salt and pepper
75 g (3 oz) pine nuts or flaked almonds, roasted and chopped
10 ml (2 tsp) soy sauce
30 ml (2 tbsp) polunsaturated oil

1 Cut a 2.5 cm (1 inch) lid from the stem end of the peppers. Scoop out the seeds and membrane. Blanch the shells and lids in boiling water for about 2 minutes. Drain and cool.

2 Melt the butter or margarine in a saucepan and gently fry the onion for 5 minutes until softened. Stir in the rice and cook for 1–2 minutes.

3 Add the stock, tomato purée and mushrooms. Bring to the boil and simmer for 30–35 minutes until the rice is tender and all the stock absorbed.

4 Season with salt and pepper to taste and stir in the nuts and soy sauce. Use this mixture to fill the peppers.

5 Replace lids, then place peppers in a deep ovenproof dish and pour over the oil. Cover and cook at 190°C (375°F) mark 5 for 30 minutes until tender.

Accompanying Vegetables

These accompanying vegetable recipes will complement a main course. Vegetables should always be as fresh as possible and never overcooked, to retain as much of their nutritional value as possible. Several recipes using pulses to serve as an accompaniment can be found here. Other pulse recipes can also be found in the Lunches, Suppers and Snacks chapter and could happily be served as an accompaniment. Try Barbecued Beans (see page 82) or Red Kidney Beans with Ginger and Chilli (see page 76). Many of the recipes here could also make an excellent starter, such as Ratatouille, served hot or cold, or Onion Bhajjias.

HOT POTATOES WITH DILL

Serves 6

900 g (2 lb) potatoes
salt and pepper
4 spring onions, finely chopped
15 ml (1 tbsp) chopped fresh dill and a sprig, to garnish
150 ml (¼ pint) soured cream

1 Place the potatoes in a saucepan of cold salted water. Bring to the boil and cook for 12–15 minutes until tender. Drain, leave until just cool enough to handle, then remove the skins.

2 Cut the potatoes into small dice and place in a bowl. Add the chopped spring onions with the chopped dill and salt and pepper to taste.

3 Thin the soured cream, if necessary, with a little boiling water or milk, stir into the potatoes and toss gently. Leave to stand for a few minutes so that the flavours blend. To serve, garnish with a sprig of dill.

Hot Potatoes with Dill

CABBAGE WITH CARAWAY

Serves 6

1.4 kg (3 lb) green cabbage
salt and pepper
50 g (2 oz) butter or polyunsaturated margarine
5 ml (1 tsp) caraway seeds

1 Shred the cabbage finely, discarding core and any tough outer leaves. Wash well under cold running water.

2 Cook in a large pan of boiling salted water for 2 minutes only – the cabbage should retain its crispness and texture. Drain well.

3 Melt the butter or margarine in the saucepan; add the drained cabbage with the caraway seeds and salt and pepper to taste. Stir over a moderate heat for 2–3 minutes until the cabbage is really hot. Taste and adjust seasoning and serve immediately.

TURNIPS IN CURRY CREAM SAUCE

Serves 4

700 g (1½ lb) small turnips, peeled
salt and pepper
50 g (2 oz) butter or polyunsaturated margarine
1 medium onion, skinned and finely chopped
100 g (4 oz) cooking apple
50 g (2 oz) sultanas
5 ml (1 tsp) mild curry powder
5 ml (1 tsp) plain wholemeal flour
150 ml (¼ pint) dry cider
150 ml (¼ pint) single cream
10 ml (2 tsp) lemon juice

1 Boil the turnips in salted water for 10–15 minutes until just tender. Meanwhile, melt the butter or margarine in a saucepan and add the onion. Cover and cook gently for 10 minutes until soft and tinged with colour. Peel and finely chop the apple and add to the onion, with the sultanas, curry powder and flour. Cook, stirring constantly, for 3–4 minutes.

2 Pour the cider into the pan, bring to the boil, then bubble gently for 2 minutes, stirring. Off the heat stir in the cream, lemon juice and salt and pepper to taste. Keep warm without boiling.

3 Drain the turnips, place in a heated dish, pour over the sauce and serve at once.

PEPPERED CARROTS

Serves 4

50 g (2 oz) butter or polyunsaturated margarine
5 ml (1 tsp) raw cane sugar
450 g (1 lb) carrots, peeled or scrubbed and thinly sliced
3 spring onions, washed and trimmed
1.25 ml (¼ tsp) cayenne pepper or to taste
45 ml (3 tbsp) soured cream
salt and pepper

1 Melt the butter or margarine with the sugar in a deep frying pan which has a tightly fitting lid. Put the carrots into the pan, cover tightly and cook gently for 10–15 minutes until tender.

2 Remove the lid from the pan and snip in the spring onions with a pair of sharp kitchen scissors. Transfer carrots and onions with a slotted spoon to a serving dish and keep warm.

3 Stir the cayenne pepper and soured cream into the pan. Taste and adjust seasoning, and warm through for 1–2 minutes. Pour over the carrots and serve.

FRENCH BEANS IN SOURED CREAM WITH PAPRIKA

Serves 4

700 g (1½ lb) French beans
25 g (1 oz) butter or polyunsaturated margarine
1 small onion, skinned and chopped
5 ml (1 tsp) paprika
150 ml (¼ pint) stock
salt and pepper
150 ml (¼ pint) soured cream

1 Using kitchen scissors, top and tail the French beans and cut them into 2.5 ml (1 inch) lengths. Melt the butter or margarine in a pan, add the onion and cook gently for 5 minutes until soft and golden.

2 Stir in 2.5 ml (½ tsp) paprika, the beans, stock and salt and pepper to taste. Bring to the boil, cover and simmer for 5–10 minutes until the French beans are tender.

3 Stir the soured cream into the pan and reheat without boiling. Turn into a heated serving dish and dust the top with the remaining paprika.

CHINESE STIR-FRY

SERVES 6

450 g (1 lb) broccoli
350 g (12 oz) carrots, peeled
4 large courgettes, trimmed
salt and pepper
30 ml (2 tbsp) sesame seed oil
1 large onion, skinned and finely chopped
3 garlic cloves, skinned and crushed
2.5 cm (1 inch) piece of fresh root ginger, peeled and crushed
225 g (8 oz) beansprouts
45 ml (3 tbsp) soy sauce
30 ml (2 tbsp) clear honey
15 ml (1 tbsp) red wine vinegar
10 ml (2 tsp) tomato purée
30 ml (2 tbsp) polyunsaturated oil

1 Cut the broccoli into bite-sized florets and the carrots into matchsticks. Blanch together in boiling salted water for 2 minutes. Remove and set aside.

2 Cut the courgettes into thin slices. Add to the pan, bring the water back to the boil and blanch for 1 minute only. Drain, reserving 60 ml (4 tbsp) of the water, and set aside.

3 Heat the sesame seed oil in a wok or large, deep frying pan. Add the onion, garlic and ginger and fry gently until soft and lightly coloured. Add the beansprouts and stir-fry for 2 minutes only. Remove with a slotted spoon and set aside until ready to serve.

4 In a jug or bowl, mix the reserved blanching water with the soy sauce, honey, vinegar and tomato purée.

5 Heat the oil in the wok, add the blanched vegetables and stir-fry for 2 minutes or until heated through.

6 Pour in the soy sauce mixture and add the beansprouts. Stir-fry for 1–2 minutes until very hot. Add salt and pepper to taste, turn into a warmed serving dish and serve immediately.

Chinese Stir Fry

GREEN BEANS WITH COCONUT

SERVES 6

700 g (1½ lb) fresh or frozen green beans or mange-tout
salt and pepper
1 medium onion, skinned
50 g (2 oz) butter or polyunsaturated margarine
50 g (2 oz) desiccated coconut
45 ml (3 tbsp) chopped fresh parsley

1 Cook the fresh beans in boiling salted water for 10 minutes, or 3 minutes for fresh mange-tout (for frozen vegetables, follow packet instructions), until cooked but firm to the bite.

2 Meanwhile, finely chop the onion. Heat the butter or margarine in a small frying pan, add the onion and cook gently until softened, stirring occasionally.

3 Increase the heat, add the coconut and fry for 2–3 minutes until golden. Season with salt and pepper to taste and mix in parsley. Drain the beans, spoon into a serving dish and sprinkle over coconut mixture.

CUCUMBER WITH ROSEMARY

SERVES 4–6

1 medium cucumber
salt and pepper
50 g (2 oz) butter or polyunsaturated margarine
1 small onion, skinned and finely chopped
15 ml (1 tbsp) chopped fresh rosemary
2.5 ml (½ tsp) raw cane sugar
60 ml (4 tbsp) soured cream

1 Score the cucumber. Cut into 5 cm (2 inch) lengths, then cut each lengthways into quarters. Remove seeds. Put in a colander and sprinkle with salt. Cover with a plate and leave for 30 minutes. Press to extract liquid, rinse and pat dry with absorbent kitchen paper.

2 Melt the butter or margarine in a frying pan. Add the onion and fry for 5 minutes. Add the cucumber, rosemary, sugar and pepper to taste and fry for 5 minutes only, stirring. Remove from the heat and stir in the soured cream. Serve hot.

Green Beans with Coconut

Cucumber with Rosemary

CAULIFLOWER IN CURRY SAUCE

Serves 4

1 large cauliflower
90 ml (6 tbsp) ghee or polyunsaturated oil
5 ml (1 tsp) black mustard seeds
5 ml (1 tsp) cumin seeds
5 cm (2 inch) piece of fresh root ginger, peeled and finely chopped
1 small onion, skinned and finely chopped
5 ml (1 tsp) salt
5 ml (1 tsp) turmeric
3 tomatoes, skinned and finely chopped
1 small green chilli, seeded and finely chopped
2.5 ml (½ tsp) raw cane sugar
30 ml (2 tbsp) chopped fresh coriander

1 Divide the cauliflower into small florets, discarding the green leaves and tough stalks. Wash the florets well and dry on absorbent kitchen paper.

2 Heat the ghee or oil in a heavy-based saucepan or flameproof casserole. Add the mustard seeds and, when they begin to pop, stir in the cumin seeds, ginger, onion, salt and turmeric. Fry for 2–3 minutes, stirring constantly.

3 Add the cauliflower and mix well to coat with the spice mixture. Stir in the tomatoes, chopped green chilli, sugar and half the coriander. Cover the pan tightly and cook gently for 15 minutes or until the cauliflower is tender but not mushy.

4 Uncover the casserole and boil rapidly for 1–2 minutes to thicken the sauce. Turn into a warmed serving dish and sprinkle with the remaining chopped coriander. Serve immediately.

ONIONS À LA GRECQUE

Serves 8

900 g (2 lb) small pickling onions
75 ml (5 tbsp) olive oil
15 ml (1 tbsp) clear honey
300 ml (½ pint) water
150 ml (¼ pint) dry white wine
10 ml (2 tsp) tomato purée
salt and pepper
100 g (4 oz) seedless raisins
30 ml (2 tbsp) chopped fresh coriander or parsley

Cauliflower in Curry Sauce

1 To skin the onions, blanch in boiling water for 1 minute only, then drain and rinse under cold running water. Remove the onion skins carefully with your fingers and a small, sharp knife.

2 Put the onions in a large, heavy-based pan with the remaining ingredients except for the raisins and chopped coriander, adding salt and pepper to taste. Bring to the boil, then lower the heat, cover and simmer gently for 30 minutes.

3 Add the raisins to the pan and continue cooking, uncovered, for a further 15 minutes or until onions are tender but still whole. Taste and adjust seasoning, then stir in the chopped coriander. Turn into a warmed serving dish and serve hot.

CRUNCHY CABBAGE

Serves 6

350 g (12 oz) red cabbage
225 g (8 oz) cooked beetroot, skinned
1 medium onion, skinned and thinly sliced
about 30 ml (2 tbsp) peanut or polyunsaturated oil
30 ml (2 tbsp) creamed horseradish
salt and pepper

1 Finely shred the red cabbage, discarding the core and any thick, woody stalks. Coarsely grate the beetroot or, if preferred, chop finely.

2 Heat 30 ml (2 tbsp) oil in a wok or large frying pan until smoking. Stir in the cabbage and onion. Cook over high heat for 3–4 minutes, stirring all the time, until the cabbage has softened a little but still retains its crispness. Add a little more oil if necessary.

3 Stir in the beetroot, horseradish and salt and pepper to taste. Cook, stirring, for a further few minutes to heat through. Serve immediately.

Okra Fried with Onion and Green Chilli

Onion Bhajjias

OKRA FRIED WITH ONION AND GREEN CHILLI

Serves 4

450 g (1 lb) fresh okra or two 425 g (15 oz) cans okra in brine, drained
45 ml (3 tbsp) ghee or polyunsaturated oil
1 medium onion, skinned and finely sliced
2 small green chillies
10 ml (2 tsp) ground cumin
salt and pepper

1 Wash the fresh okra and trim the ends. Dry well on absorbent kitchen paper. If using canned okra, rinse, drain and dry well.

2 Heat the oil in a large, heavy-based frying pan or wok, add the onion and fry over moderate heat, stirring constantly, for about 5 minutes until turning golden.

3 Trim the ends off the green chillies and cut the flesh into fine rings. Remove as many seeds as you like, according to how hot the dish is to be.

4 Add the okra, chillies and cumin, with salt and pepper to taste. Continue cooking over moderate heat, stirring constantly, for about 10–15 minutes. The fresh okra should be cooked but still quite crisp and the onions a deeper brown. The canned okra will become slightly sticky. Taste and adjust the seasoning, then turn into a warmed serving dish. Serve immediately.

ONION BHAJJIAS

Serves 4

150 g (5 oz) gram flour (chick pea flour)
5 ml (1 tsp) bicarbonate of soda
salt and pepper
10 ml (2 tsp) coriander seeds, crushed
2.5 ml (½ tsp) garam masala
5 ml (1 tsp) turmeric
5 ml (1 tsp) chilli powder
4 green cardamoms
30 ml (2 tbsp) chopped fresh mint or coriander
2 large onions, skinned and chopped
polyunsaturated oil, for deep frying
lemon or lime wedges, to garnish

1 Sift the flour, bicarbonate of soda and 10 ml (2 tsp) salt into a bowl. Mix in the coriander seeds, garam masala, turmeric and chilli powder.

2 Open the cardamom pods and take out the seeds. Discard the husks and crush the seeds lightly. Add to the flour mixture with the fresh mint or coriander, onion, salt and pepper to taste and 30 ml (2 tbsp) water. Mix to a fairly stiff paste.

3 Heat the oil in a deep-fat frier to 180°C (350°F). Using 2 wet dessert spoons, drop 6 spoonfuls of the mixture at a time into the hot oil and deep fry for 3–4 minutes or until darkish brown in colour. Remove with a slotted spoon and drain on absorbent kitchen paper. Serve piping hot, with lemon or lime wedges.

SAUTÉED AUBERGINES WITH MUSTARD SEEDS AND YOGURT

SERVES 6

3 medium aubergines, total weight about 900 g (2 lb)
60 ml (4 tbsp) ghee or polyunsaturated oil
30 ml (2 tbsp) black mustard seeds, ground
2.5 ml (½ tsp) chilli powder
60 ml (4 tbsp) chopped fresh coriander
5 ml (1 tsp) salt
300 ml (½ pint) natural yogurt

1 Grill the aubergines for about 15 minutes, turning occasionally, until the skins are charred and the flesh soft. Leave until just cool enough to handle, then peel off the skins and discard. Chop the flesh roughly and set aside.

2 Heat the ghee or oil in a heavy-based frying pan. Add the ground mustard seeds, aubergine flesh and the chilli powder. Stir over moderate heat for about 5 minutes or until thoroughly hot, then add the coriander.

3 Beat the salt into the yogurt, then stir into the aubergine until evenly blended. Turn into a warmed serving dish and serve immediately.

CREAMED BROCCOLI BAKE

SERVES 6

700 g (1½ lb) broccoli
450 ml (¾ pint) milk
salt and pepper
50 g (2 oz) butter or polyunsaturated margarine
60 ml (4 tbsp) plain wholemeal flour
1.25 ml (¼ tsp) freshly grated nutmeg
2 eggs, separated
25 g (1 oz) fresh wholemeal breadcrumbs

1 Trim and discard any thick broccoli stems. Cut up the florets into small pieces, then wash and drain well. Put in a medium saucepan with the milk and seasoning and bring to the boil. Cover the pan tightly and simmer gently for 10–15 minutes.

2 Strain off the milk and reserve, then finely chop the cooked broccoli. Rinse out and dry the saucepan, then melt the butter or margarine and stir in the flour. Cook for 1–2 minutes. Gradually stir in the reserved milk (there should be about 300 ml/½ pint), season with salt and pepper to taste and bring to the boil. Bubble for 2 minutes, stirring.

3 Remove from the heat, beat in the broccoli, nutmeg and egg yolks, taste and adjust seasoning.

4 Whisk the egg whites until stiff and fold into the sauce. Spoon into a well greased 1.4 litre (2½ pint) shallow ovenproof dish.

5 Scatter the breadcrumbs over the top, and bake at 170°C (325°F) mark 3 for about 50 minutes or until the topping has just set. Serve immediately.

Sautéed Aubergines with Mustard Seeds and Yogurt

COURGETTES WITH MUSHROOMS

SERVES 6

1.1 kg (2½ lb) courgettes, trimmed
50 g (2 oz) butter or polyunsaturated margarine
salt and pepper
225 g (8 oz) button mushrooms
150 ml (¼ pint) soured cream
fresh basil sprig, to garnish

1 Slice the courgettes into 0.5 cm (¼ inch) pieces. Melt the butter or margarine in a medium roasting tin, add the courgettes and turn over in the butter or margarine. Season with salt and pepper to taste.

Courgettes with Mushrooms

2 Bake the courgette slices at 200°C (400°F) mark 6 for about 20 minutes.

3 Meanwhile, slice the mushrooms. Stir into the courgettes and return to the oven for a further 10–15 minutes.

4 Stir the soured cream and then mix through the vegetables; bubble up on top of the cooker. To serve, adjust seasoning and spoon the vegetables into a serving dish. Garnish with the basil.

WATERCRESS AND OATMEAL CROQUETTES

MAKES 12

700 g (1½ lb) floury potatoes
15 g (½ oz) butter or polyunsaturated margarine, softened
1 bunch watercress
2 eggs
salt and pepper
15 ml (1 tbsp) plain wholemeal flour
50 g (2 oz) fresh wholemeal breadcrumbs
50 g (2 oz) medium oatmeal
polyunsaturated oil, for deep frying

1 Scrub the potatoes and boil in their skins until tender, about 20 minutes. Drain well, peel, then sieve them into a large bowl or mash very well. Beat in the butter or margarine.

2 Wash, drain and finely chop the watercress. Add to the bowl with 1 egg and salt and pepper to taste; mix well. Mould the potato mixture into 12 cork-shaped croquettes. Coat each lightly in flour.

3 Break the remaining egg on to a plate and beat lightly. Combine the breadcrumbs and oatmeal on another plate.

4 Brush the croquettes with the beaten egg, then coat in the breadcrumb mixture, pressing it on firmly. Chill for at least 30 minutes or until required.

5 To serve, heat the oil in a deep fat frier to 190°C (375°F). Deep fry the croquettes for about 4 minutes or until golden brown on all sides. Drain on absorbent kitchen paper before serving.

TOMATOES AU GRATIN

SERVES 6

900 g (2 lb) large Continental tomatoes
50 g (2 oz) butter or polyunsaturated margarine, softened
2–3 garlic cloves, skinned and chopped
5 ml (1 tsp) raw cane sugar
20 ml (4 tsp) chopped fresh basil or 10 ml (2 tsp) dried
salt and pepper
300 ml (½ pint) double cream
50 g (2 oz) dried wholemeal breadcrumbs
25 g (1 oz) freshly grated Parmesan cheese

1 Skin the tomatoes: put them in a large bowl, pour over boiling water and leave for 10 seconds. Drain, then plunge the tomatoes into a bowl of cold water. Peel off the skin with your fingers, then slice the tomatoes thinly.

2 Brush the inside of an ovenproof dish liberally with some of the butter or margarine. Arrange a layer of tomato slices in the bottom of the dish, sprinkle with a little of the garlic, sugar and basil, then add salt and pepper to taste. Pour over a thin layer of cream.

3 Repeat these layers until all the ingredients are used up. Mix the breadcrumbs and Parmesan together, then sprinkle over the top of the tomatoes and cream. Dot with the remaining butter or margarine.

4 Bake at 180°C (350°F) mark 4 for 40 minutes until the topping is golden brown. Serve hot.

RATATOUILLE

Serves 6

450 g (1 lb) aubergines
salt and pepper
450 g (1 lb) courgettes, trimmed
3 red or green peppers
120 ml (8 tbsp) olive oil
450 g (1 lb) onions, skinned and chopped
1 garlic clove, skinned and crushed
450 g (1 lb) tomatoes, skinned, seeded and chopped, or one 397 g (14 oz) can tomatoes, drained
30 ml (2 tbsp) tomato purée
bouquet garni

1 Cut the aubergines into thin slices and place in a colander or large sieve. Sprinkle with salt and set aside for 30 minutes. Rinse under cold running water and pat dry with absorbent kitchen paper.

2 Meanwhile, cut the courgettes into thin slices. Slice off the stems of the peppers and remove the seeds. Cut into thin rings.

3 Heat the oil in a large saucepan. Add the onions and garlic and cook gently for about 10 minutes until soft and golden.

4 Add the tomatoes and purée, cook for a few more minutes, then add the aubergines, courgettes, peppers, bouquet garni and salt and pepper to taste. Cover and simmer gently for 1 hour. The vegetables should be soft but retain their shape. If the cooking liquid has not evaporated, remove the lid and cook for another 20 minutes. Check the seasoning and serve hot or cold.

Ratatouille

BAKED FENNEL

Serves 6

700 g (1½ lb) fennel bulbs
salt and pepper
75 g (3 oz) butter or polyunsaturated margarine
finely grated rind of 1 large thin-skinned lemon and 30 ml (2 tbsp) fresh lemon juice

1 Trim the base and top stems of the fennel, reserving some of the feathery green tops. Quarter each head lengthways. Blanch in boiling salted water for 5 minutes.

2 Melt the butter or margarine in a shallow flameproof casserole. Remove from the heat and add the lemon rind with the lemon juice. Season with salt and pepper to taste.

3 Arrange fennel in the casserole in a single layer and turn in the butter or margarine. Cover tightly with a lid or foil and bake at 150°C (300°F) mark 2 for about 1¼ hours. Garnish with snipped fennel tops. Serve hot.

VEGETABLE STIR-FRY

SERVES 4

1 turnip, peeled
4 small carrots, peeled
4 celery sticks
2 young leeks, washed and trimmed
30 ml (2 tbsp) sesame oil
15 ml (1 tbsp) polyunsaturated oil
100 g (4 oz) beansprouts, washed and drained
10 ml (2 tsp) soy sauce
5 ml (1 tsp) white wine vinegar
5 ml (1 tsp) raw cane sugar
5 ml (1 tsp) five-spice powder
salt

1 Using a sharp knife, cut the turnip and carrots into matchstick strips. Slice the celery and leeks finely.

2 Heat the oils in a wok and add the prepared vegetables with the beansprouts. Stir-fry over moderate heat for 3–4 minutes, then sprinkle in the soy sauce, wine vinegar, sugar, five-spice powder and salt to taste. Stir-fry for 1 minute more. Serve at once, while piping hot.

NEW POTATOES WITH TARRAGON CREAM

SERVES 4

15 g (½ oz) butter or polyunsaturated margarine
4 spring onions, trimmed and chopped
150 ml (¼ pint) soured cream
salt and pepper
3 sprigs of fresh tarragon
700 g (1½ lb) cooked new potatoes, drained and kept hot

1 Melt the butter or margarine in a saucepan, add the onions and cook for 5 minutes until soft. Stir in the soured cream, salt and pepper to taste, and two tarragon sprigs. Heat without boiling.

2 Add the cooked potatoes to the creamy onion and tarragon mixture in the pan. Reheat gently, but do not boil.

3 Turn the potatoes and the sauce into a warm serving dish and serve garnished with the remaining sprig of fresh tarragon.

COLCANNON
(Irish Mashed Potatoes with Kale and Leeks)

SERVES 6

450 g (1 lb) potatoes, peeled and quartered
salt and pepper
450 g (1 lb) kale or cabbage, cored and shredded
2 small leeks, sliced and washed
150 ml (¼ pint) milk or double cream
50 g (2 oz) butter or polyunsaturated margarine
melted butter, to serve

1 Cook the potatoes in boiling salted water for 15–20 minutes until tender. Meanwhile, cook the cabbage in a pan of boiling salted water for 5–10 minutes until tender. Drain both potatoes and cabbage. Put the leeks and milk or cream in a saucepan and simmer gently for 10–15 minutes until soft.

2 In a large bowl, combine the cooked vegetables with the butter or margarine and salt and pepper to taste. Beat together over gentle heat until the mixture is a pale green mass.

3 Mound the mixture on a warmed serving dish and make a hollow in the top. Pour a little melted butter into the hollow, to be mixed in at the last minute.

Vegetable Stir-Fry

SAG ALOO

Serves 4–6

900 g (2 lb) fresh spinach or 450 g (1 lb) frozen leaf spinach, thawed and drained
60 ml (4 tbsp) ghee or polyunsaturated oil
1 medium onion, skinned and thinly sliced
2 garlic cloves, skinned and crushed
10 ml (2 tsp) ground coriander
5 ml (1 tsp) black mustard seeds
2.5 ml (½ tsp) turmeric
1.25 ml (¼ tsp) chilli powder
1.25 ml (¼ tsp) ground ginger
salt
450 g (1 lb) old potatoes, peeled and thickly sliced

1 If using fresh spinach, wash well and put in a large saucepan with only the water that clings to the leaves. Cook over very gentle heat for about 15 minutes. Drain well and leave to cool.

2 With your hands, squeeze out all the remaining moisture from the spinach. Place on a board and chop finely.

3 If using frozen spinach, cook over very gentle heat for about 5 minutes to drive off as much liquid as possible.

4 Melt the ghee or oil in a heavy-based saucepan or flameproof casserole. Add the onion, garlic, spices and salt to taste. Fry gently for about 5 minutes, stirring frequently, until the onion begins to brown.

5 Add the potatoes and stir gently to mix with the onion and spices. Pour in 150 ml (¼ pint) water and bring to the boil, then lower the heat and simmer, uncovered, for 10 minutes. Stir occasionally and add a few more spoonfuls of water if necessary.

6 Fold the spinach gently into the potato mixture. Simmer for a further 5–10 minutes until the potatoes are just tender. Turn into a warmed serving dish and serve hot.

Sag Aloo

RÖSTI

Serves 2–4

700 g (1½ lb) old potatoes, scrubbed
salt and pepper
75 g (3 oz) butter or polyunsaturated margarine
1 small onion, skinned and finely chopped

1 Quarter any large potatoes and put in a saucepan of salted water. Bring to the boil and cook for 7 minutes. Drain well, leave to cool for about 10 minutes until cool enough to handle, then remove the skins. Using a hand grater, grate the potatoes into a bowl. Melt 25 g (1 oz) of the butter or margarine in a frying pan, add the onion and fry gently for about 5 minutes until soft but not coloured.

2 Add the remaining butter or margarine to the onion and heat until melted. Add the grated potato and sprinkle with salt and pepper to taste. Fry the potatoes, turning them constantly, until they have absorbed all the fat.

3 Using a palette knife, form the potato into a neat, flat cake and flatten the top. Sprinkle with 15 ml (1 tbsp) water, cover the pan and cook gently for 15–20 minutes, until the underside is golden brown. Shake the pan occasionally to prevent the potato from sticking to the bottom of the pan.

4 When cooked, place a large warmed serving plate on top of the frying pan. Invert both so that the golden side is uppermost on the plate. Serve immediately, cut into wedges. Alternatively, serve straight from the pan, cut into wedges and inverted.

DRY MOONG DAL

SERVES 4–6

225 g (8 oz) moong dal, soaked in cold water for 4 hours
1 small onion, skinned
polyunsaturated oil, for frying
10 ml (2 tsp) ground cumin
10 ml (2 tsp) ground coriander
1.25 ml (¼ tsp) turmeric
pinch of cayenne pepper
salt

1 Put the dal into a sieve and wash thoroughly under cold running water. Pick over and remove any discoloured pulses. Set aside.

2 Cut the onion into extremely thin slices. Heat about 1 cm (½ inch) oil in a frying pan, add the onion and fry gently for about 10 minutes until golden brown. Remove from the pan with a slotted spoon and spread on absorbent kitchen paper to drain. Leave to cool.

3 Heat 30 ml (2 tbsp) oil in a large saucepan and stir in the cumin, coriander, turmeric and cayenne. Add the dal and stir together. Add 300 ml (½ pint) water and salt to taste.

4 Bring to the boil, cover and simmer for about 25–30 minutes until the dal is tender and the water absorbed.

5 Turn the dal into a warmed serving dish and sprinkle the crisp, browned onions over the top. Serve hot.

FRIED MASALA POTATOES

SERVES 4–6

900 g (2 lb) new potatoes
ghee or polyunsaturated oil, for deep frying
10 ml (2 tsp) cumin seeds
15 ml (1 tbsp) coriander seeds
7.5 ml (1½ tsp) garam masala
2.5 cm (1 inch) piece of fresh root ginger, peeled and roughly chopped
4 garlic cloves, skinned and chopped
2 medium onions, skinned and chopped
45 ml (3 tbsp) ghee or polyunsaturated oil
5 ml (1 tsp) chilli powder
2.5 ml (½ tsp) turmeric
5 ml (1 tsp) salt
300 ml (½ pint) natural yogurt

1 Wash the potatoes and scrub clean if necessary. Cut into 2.5 cm (1 inch) pieces and pat dry with absorbent kitchen paper.

2 Heat the oil in a deep-fat frier to 180°C (350°F) and deep fry the potatoes in batches for 10 minutes or until golden brown. Remove from the oil and drain on absorbent kitchen paper.

3 Place the cumin and coriander seeds in a blender or food processor with the garam masala, ginger, garlic and onions. Work until smooth, adding a little water if necessary.

4 Heat the ghee or oil in a heavy-based frying pan, add the masala paste and fry gently for about 5 minutes. Add the chilli, turmeric and salt and fry for a further 1 minute.

5 Pour in the yogurt, then add the potatoes. Stir well and cook for another 5 minutes until completely heated through. Serve piping hot.

Fried Masala Potatoes

ACCOMPANYING VEGETABLES

GRUYÈRE POTATOES

Serves 6

900 g (2 lb) potatoes
25 g (1 oz) butter or polyunsaturated margarine
125 g (4 oz) Gruyère cheese, grated
freshly grated nutmeg
salt and pepper
568 ml (1 pint) milk

1 Peel the potatoes, then slice thinly. (Do not soak them in cold water.) Use a little of the butter or margarine to lightly grease a 1.4 litre (2½ pint) shallow ovenproof dish.

2 Layer the potatoes and most of the cheese in the dish. Add a generous grating of nutmeg and salt and pepper to taste. Top with cheese and pour over the milk, which should just cover the potatoes.

3 Dot the surface with the remaining butter or margarine. Cover with foil and bake at 180°C (350°F) mark 4 for about 1½ hours or until the potatoes are quite tender, most of the milk has been absorbed and the top is golden brown. Serve hot.

4 Bake at 180°C (350°F) mark 4 for 45 minutes until the top is golden brown. Serve hot.

DHAL
(Lentil Purée)

Serves 4

100 g (4 oz) red lentils
30 ml (2 tbsp) polyunsaturated oil
1 medium onion, skinned and finely chopped
25 g (1 oz) butter or polyunsaturated margarine
salt and pepper

1 Rinse the lentils and put in a saucepan with 300 ml (½ pint) cold water. Bring to the boil and simmer for about 1 hour until tender, adding more water if they get too dry.

2 Meanwhile, heat the oil in a pan, add the onion and fry for 5 minutes until soft.

3 When the lentils are tender, remove from the heat and stir vigorously to form a purée. Add the butter or margarine and fried onion and stir over the heat. Season with salt and pepper to taste and serve hot.

CHANA DAL

Serves 4

225 g (8 oz) chana dal
15 ml (1 tbsp) whole black peppercorns
60 ml (4 tbsp) ghee or polyunsaturated oil
1 medium onion, skinned and chopped
25 g (1 oz) fresh root ginger, peeled and finely chopped
1 garlic clove, skinned and crushed
10 ml (2 tsp) turmeric
about 1 litre (1¾ pints) vegetable stock
salt

1 Pick over the dal and remove any grit or discoloured pulses. Put into a sieve and wash thoroughly under cold running water. Drain well. Crush the peppercorns with a pestle and mortar.

2 Heat the ghee or oil in a heavy-based saucepan, add the onion and fry gently for about 5 minutes until soft and lightly coloured. Stir in the ginger, garlic, turmeric, peppercorns and dal. Stir over gentle heat for 2–3 minutes.

3 Add the stock and bring to the boil. Cover and simmer for about 1 hour, stirring frequently until the dal is tender and quite mushy in consistency. Add salt to taste before serving.

Gruyère Potatoes

SALADS AND DRESSINGS

In this chapter you will find both salads to serve as a meal on their own and side salads to accompany a main dish. Serve substantial salads with wholemeal or granary bread, or for a change make a batch of Cheese Scones (see page 159) or in winter accompany with a baked potato. At the end of this chapter you will find a wide variety of dressings, from French Dressing and Mayonnaise to the more unusual Soured Cream and Watercress Dressing, in which to toss your salad.

AVOCADO AND LEMON SALAD WITH OMELETTE RINGS

SERVES 4–6 AS A MAIN MEAL

4 eggs
50 g (2 oz) Cheddar cheese, grated
salt and pepper
25 g (1 oz) butter or polyunsaturated margarine
5 ml (1 tsp) whole black peppercorns
5 ml (1 tsp) whole coriander seeds
90 ml (6 tbsp) olive oil
45 ml (3 tbsp) lemon juice
2 ripe avocados
parsley sprigs, to garnish (optional)

1 Put the eggs in a bowl with the cheese, 15 ml (1 tbsp) water and salt and pepper to taste. Whisk together.

2 Melt a quarter of the butter or margarine in an omelette pan or small non-stick frying pan. When foaming, pour in a quarter of the egg mixture. After a few seconds, push the set egg mixture into the centre of the pan to allow the uncooked egg to run to the edges. Cook until just set.

3 Brown the omelette under a preheated hot grill. Turn out on to a plate. Repeat with remaining egg mixture to make another 3 omelettes. While the omelettes are still warm, roll them up loosely. Wrap in greaseproof paper and leave to cool.

4 Meanwhile, crush the peppercorns and coriander seeds coarsely with a pestle and mortar, or with the end of a rolling pin in a sturdy bowl.

5 In a bowl, whisk together the oil, lemon juice, crushed spices and salt and pepper to taste. Halve, stone and peel the avocados, then slice thickly into the dressing. Toss gently to coat completely.

6 Slice the omelettes thinly. Arrange the omelette rings and avocado slices on individual serving plates. Spoon over the dressing and garnish with sprigs of parsley, if liked. Serve immediately.

Avocado and Lemon Salad with Omelette Rings

Winter Cabbage and Cauliflower Salad

GREEK SALAD

SERVES 4 AS A MAIN MEAL

2 large tomatoes
1 green pepper
½ medium cucumber
50 g (2 oz) black olives
225 g (8 oz) Feta cheese
120 ml (8 tbsp) olive oil
30–45 ml (2–3 tbsp) lemon juice
salt and pepper
large pinch of dried oregano
pitta bread, to serve

1 Using a sharp knife, cut each tomato in half. Then cut each of the halves into four equal wedges. Halve, seed and slice the green pepper thinly.

2 Cut the cucumber half into thick slices. Stone the olives. Arrange the tomato wedges, sliced pepper and cucumber and the olives in a salad bowl.

3 Dice the cheese and add to the bowl, reserving a few dice for garnish. Pour over the olive oil, followed by the lemon juice and season with salt and pepper to taste.

4 Toss the salad well together. Crumble over the remaining cheese cubes, sprinkle with oregano and serve with pitta bread.

WINTER CABBAGE AND CAULIFLOWER SALAD

SERVES 4 AS A SIDE SALAD

225 g (8 oz) hard white cabbage
225 g (8 oz) cauliflower florets
2 large carrots, peeled
75 g (3 oz) mixed shelled nuts, roughly chopped
50 g (2 oz) raisins
60 ml (4 tbsp) chopped fresh parsley or coriander
30 ml (2 tbsp) mayonnaise
60 ml (4 tbsp) soured cream or natural yogurt
10 ml (2 tsp) French mustard
30 ml (2 tbsp) olive oil
juice of ½ lemon
salt and pepper
3 red-skinned eating apples

1 Shred the cabbage finely with a sharp knife and place in a large bowl. Divide the cauliflower florets into small sprigs and add to the cabbage. Mix gently with your hands.

2 Grate the carrots into the bowl, then add the nuts, raisins and parsley. Mix the vegetables together again until evenly combined.

3 Put the remaining ingredients except the apples in a jug. Whisk well to combine, then pour over the vegetables in the bowl and toss well.

4 Core and chop the apples, but do not peel them. Add to the salad and toss again to combine with the other ingredients. Cover the bowl and chill the salad for about 1 hour before serving. With extra nuts, this salad would make a meal in itself, served with cheese and wholemeal or granary bread.

WHOLEWHEAT BRAZIL SALAD

SERVES 4–6 AS A MAIN MEAL

75 g (3 oz) dried black-eyed beans, soaked in cold water overnight
100 g (4 oz) wholewheat grain, soaked in cold water overnight
90 ml (6 tbsp) natural yogurt
30 ml (2 tbsp) olive oil
45 ml (3 tbsp) lemon juice
45 ml (3 tbsp) chopped fresh mint
salt and pepper
½ cucumber, diced
225 g (8 oz) tomatoes, skinned and roughly chopped
100 g (4 oz) Cheddar cheese, grated
100 g (4 oz) Brazil nuts, roughly chopped
lettuce leaves and mint sprigs, to garnish

1 Drain the beans and place in a saucepan of water. Bring to the boil and simmer gently for 1½ hours or until tender.

2 Meanwhile, drain the wholewheat and place in a saucepan of water. Bring to the boil and simmer gently for 20–25 minutes or until tender. Drain, rinse well with cold water and cool for 30 minutes. When the beans are cooked, drain and cool for 30 minutes.

3 Whisk the yogurt and olive oil together with the lemon juice, mint and salt and pepper to taste.

4 Put the wholewheat, beans, cucumber, tomatoes, cheese and Brazil nuts in a bowl. Pour over the dressing and mix well.

5 Line a salad bowl with lettuce leaves and pile the wholewheat salad on top. Chill before serving, then garnish with mint sprigs.

Wholewheat Brazil Salad

SPINACH AND MUSHROOM SALAD

SERVES 6 AS A MAIN MEAL

225 g (8 oz) fresh spinach, washed and trimmed
2 large slices of wholemeal bread
polyunsaturated oil, for frying
2 oranges
10 ml (2 tsp) wholegrain mustard
1 garlic clove, skinned and crushed (optional)
90 ml (6 tbsp) polyunsaturated oil
30 ml (2 tbsp) lemon juice
salt and pepper
2 avocados
225 g (8 oz) button mushrooms, sliced

1 Shred the spinach leaves into small strips and place in a bowl. Set aside.

2 Cut the crusts off the bread, then cut it into 5 mm (¼ inch) cubes or into shapes. Pour oil into a frying pan to just cover the base, and fry the bread until browned. Drain on absorbent kitchen paper.

3 Peel the oranges using a serrated knife, cutting away all the skin and pith. Cut the oranges into segments, removing the membrane.

4 Whisk together the mustard, garlic, oil, lemon juice and salt and pepper to taste until emulsified.

5 Halve the avocados and remove the stones. Peel, then chop the flesh into chunks.

6 Place the oranges, avocados and mushrooms on top of the spinach and pour over the dressing. Mix together carefully and sprinkle with the croûtons. Serve immediately.

TURMERIC AND WALNUT MUSHROOMS

SERVES 8 AS A MAIN MEAL

1.1 kg (2½ lb) button mushrooms
300 ml (½ pint) olive oil
100 ml (4 fl oz) white wine vinegar
5 ml (1 tsp) Dijon mustard
5 ml (1 tsp) raw cane sugar
15 ml (1 tbsp) turmeric
1 garlic clove, skinned and crushed
salt and pepper
125 g (4 oz) walnut pieces
350 g (12 oz) Emmental cheese, cubed
chopped fresh parsley, to garnish

1 Wipe the button mushrooms. Leave the small ones whole and cut any larger ones in half. Place in a serving dish.

2 In a jug, whisk together the oil, vinegar, mustard, sugar, turmeric and garlic until well blended. Add salt and pepper to taste.

3 Pour the dressing over the mushrooms and mix thoroughly to coat. Cover and leave to marinate in the refrigerator for at least 8 hours.

4 To serve, stir the mushrooms well and mix in the walnut pieces and Emmental. Garnish with chopped parsley.

GRAPE, WATERCRESS AND STILTON SALAD

SERVES 4 AS A MAIN MEAL

175 g (6 oz) black grapes
1 bunch watercress
45 ml (3 tbsp) polyunsaturated oil
15 ml (1 tbsp) lemon juice
5 ml (1 tsp) poppy seeds
pinch of raw cane sugar
salt and pepper
225 g (8 oz) Stilton cheese

1 Halve the grapes and remove the pips. Place in a bowl, cover and chill in the refrigerator. Trim the watercress of any tough root ends. Wash thoroughly, drain well and pat dry with absorbent kitchen paper.

2 In a jug, whisk together the oil, lemon juice, poppy seeds, sugar and salt and pepper to taste.

3 Cut the rind off the Stilton and cut the cheese into 1.5 cm (¾ inch) cubes. Toss well in the prepared dressing to coat completely. Cover and chill for 1 hour.

4 To serve, toss together the grapes, watercress, Stilton and dressing. Serve immediately.

Spinach and Mushroom Salad

CHEESE, BEANSPROUT AND PINEAPPLE SALAD

Serves 4 as a main meal

275 g (10 oz) beansprouts
225 g (8 oz) carrots, peeled
225 g (8 oz) Edam cheese or tofu (see page 109)
227 g (8 oz) can pineapple slices in natural juice
10 ml (2 tsp) wine vinegar
salt and pepper

1 Wash the beansprouts and drain well. Cut the carrots into 2.5 cm (1 inch) matchstick strips. Grate the cheese coarsely. Drain the pineapple, reserving the juice, and cut into thin strips.

2 In a large bowl, mix together the beansprouts, carrot, cheese and pineapple. Cover and chill until required.

3 Make the dressing. Whisk the pineapple juice and vinegar together with salt and pepper to taste.

4 Just before serving, pour the dressing over the salad and toss well to mix. Serve at room temperature.

Cheese, Beansprout and Pineapple Salad

ONION AND TOMATO RAITA

SERVES 4–6 AS A SIDE SALAD

2 firm tomatoes
1 medium onion, skinned
568 ml (1 pint) natural yogurt, well chilled
15 ml (1 tbsp) finely chopped fresh mint
2.5 ml (½ tsp) chilli powder
pinch of ground cumin
salt and pepper
15 ml (1 tbsp) chopped coriander leaves, to garnish

1 Cut the tomatoes into quarters, remove the pulp and finely chop the flesh. Finely chop the onion.

2 Put the yogurt in a bowl and stir in the tomato and onion with the mint, chilli powder and cumin. Season with salt and pepper to taste.

3 Serve garnished with chopped coriander leaves. Accompany with poppadoms, if liked.

ENDIVE, ORANGE AND WALNUT SALAD

SERVES 8 AS A SIDE SALAD

2 endives
6 oranges
25 g (1 oz) walnut pieces
15 ml (1 tbsp) raw cane sugar
150 ml (¼ pint) soured cream
60 ml (4 tbsp) polyunsaturated oil
30 ml (2 tbsp) lemon juice
salt and pepper

1 Pull the endives apart, wash and dry thoroughly. Tear into pieces and place in a salad bowl. Grate the rind of one orange into a bowl and squeeze in the juice.

2 Remove peel and white pith from remaining oranges. Segment oranges and add segments to endive. Add the walnuts.

3 Just before serving, combine the sugar, soured cream, reserved orange juice and rind. Beat in the oil gradually and stir in the lemon juice. Season with salt and pepper to taste. Spoon dressing over endives, oranges and walnuts and toss together lightly.

THREE BEAN SALAD

SERVES 4–6 AS A SIDE SALAD

75 g (3 oz) dried red kidney beans, soaked in cold water overnight
75 g (3 oz) dried black-eyed beans, soaked in cold water overnight
75 g (3 oz) dried pinto or borlotti beans, soaked in cold water overnight
100 ml (4 fl oz) French dressing (see page 155)
15 ml (1 tbsp) chopped fresh coriander
1 small onion, skinned and sliced into rings
salt and pepper
sprig of fresh coriander, to garnish

1. Drain the beans and put in a saucepan of water. Bring to the boil and boil rapidly for 10 minutes, then boil gently for 1½ hours until tender.

2. Drain the cooked beans thoroughly and place them in a large salad bowl.

3. Combine the French dressing and coriander, and pour over the beans while they are still warm.

4. Toss thoroughly and leave to cool for 30 minutes. Mix the onion into the beans, add salt and pepper to taste and chill for 2–3 hours before serving garnished with fresh coriander.

RADICCHIO AND ALFALFA SALAD

SERVES 4–6 AS A SIDE SALAD

2 heads of radicchio
50–75 g (2–3 oz) alfalfa sprouts
90 ml (6 tbsp) olive oil
30 ml (2 tbsp) white wine vinegar
15 ml (1 tbsp) single cream (optional)
1 small garlic clove, skinned and crushed
salt and pepper

1. Tear the radicchio into bite-sized pieces. Wash, drain and pat dry on absorbent kitchen paper. Wash and dry the alfalfa sprouts.

2. Mix the alfalfa and radicchio together in a serving bowl. In a jug, whisk together the remaining ingredients, with salt and pepper to taste. Just before serving, pour over the radicchio and alfalfa and toss together.

Three Bean Salad

FENNEL WITH GREEN PEPPERCORN DRESSING

SERVES 6 AS A SIDE SALAD

3 fennel bulbs
salt and pepper
15–30 ml (1–2 tbsp) lemon juice
150 ml (¼ pint) whipping cream
15 ml (1 tbsp) green peppercorns
10 ml (2 tsp) white wine or tarragon vinegar

1. Trim any green leafy tops from the fennel and reserve. Cook the fennel in plenty of boiling salted water, to which the lemon juice has been added, for 30–35 minutes or until just tender.

2. Drain well, then rinse immediately under cold running water. Cool completely; about 20 minutes. Cover and chill.

3. Whip the cream until standing in soft peaks. Roughly crush or chop the peppercorns, then fold them into the cream with the vinegar and salt and pepper to taste. Cover and chill.

4. To serve, split the fennel bulbs in half and place on a flat serving dish. Spoon over the dressing and garnish with reserved snipped fennel tops.

TOMATO AND OKRA VINAIGRETTE

SERVES 8 AS A SIDE SALAD

450 g (1 lb) okra
150 ml (¼ pint) polyunsaturated oil
30 ml (2 tbsp) lemon juice
5 ml (1 tsp) tomato purée
pinch of raw cane sugar
salt and pepper
450 g (1 lb) tomatoes, skinned

1. Trim off the tops and tails of the okra. Cook in boiling salted water for about 4 minutes or until just tender. Drain well and place in a bowl.

2. In a jug whisk together the oil, lemon juice, tomato purée, sugar and salt and pepper to taste. Pour over the warm okra and fold gently to mix.

3. Slice the tomatoes thinly. Arrange in a serving bowl with the okra and vinaigrette. Cover and chill for at least 30 minutes before serving.

WALDORF SALAD

SERVES 4 AS A SIDE SALAD

450 g (1 lb) eating apples
juice of 1 lemon
5 ml (1 tsp) raw cane sugar
150 ml (¼ pint) mayonnaise
½ head celery, trimmed and sliced
50 g (2 oz) walnuts, chopped
1 lettuce
a few walnut halves, to garnish (optional)

1 Core the apples, but do not peel. Slice one and dice the rest. Dip the slices in the lemon juice to prevent discoloration of the fruit.

2 Toss the diced apples in 30 ml (2 tbsp) lemon juice, the sugar and 15 ml (1 tbsp) mayonnaise. Leave to stand for about 30 minutes.

3 Just before serving, add the sliced celery, chopped walnuts and the remaining mayonnaise, and toss together.

4 Serve the salad in a bowl lined with lettuce leaves and garnish with the apple slices and a few walnut halves, if liked.

FENNEL AND CUCUMBER SALAD

SERVES 4 AS A SIDE SALAD

½ or 1 small cucumber
2 small fennel bulbs
90 ml (6 tbsp) olive oil
30 ml (2 tbsp) lemon juice
1 garlic clove, skinned and crushed
15 ml (1 tbsp) chopped fresh mint
pinch of raw cane sugar
salt and pepper
sliced large radishes or tomatoes, to serve

1 Peel the cucumber and halve lengthways. Scoop out the seeds and discard. Dice the flesh.

2 Trim the fennel, reserving a few feathery tops for the garnish. Grate the fennel into a bowl, add the diced cucumber and mix together.

3 Whisk together the remaining ingredients (except radishes or tomatoes). Add salt and pepper to taste. Pour over the fennel and cucumber and toss.

4 Line a shallow serving dish with radish or tomato slices then pile the salad in the centre. Garnish with reserved fennel tops.

Waldorf Salad **Fennel and Cucumber Salad**

CELERIAC AND BEAN SALAD

Serves 4–6 as a side salad

225 g (8 oz) dried flageolet beans, soaked in cold water overnight
1 large green pepper
finely grated rind and juice of 1 lemon
60 ml (4 tbsp) olive oil
15 ml (1 tbsp) whole grain mustard
1 garlic clove, skinned and crushed
45 ml (3 tbsp) chopped fresh parsley
salt and pepper
225 g (8 oz) celeriac

1 Drain the soaked beans and rinse well under cold running water. Put the beans in a large saucepan and cover with plenty of fresh cold water. Bring slowly to the boil, then skim off any scum with a slotted spoon. Half cover the pan with a lid and simmer gently for about 1 hour, or until the beans are just tender.

2 Meanwhile, halve the pepper and remove the core and seeds. Cut the flesh into strips and then into cubes. In a bowl, whisk together the grated lemon rind, about 30 ml (2 tbsp) lemon juice, the oil, mustard, garlic, parsley and salt and pepper to taste.

3 Just before the beans are ready, peel the celeriac and chop roughly into 2.5 cm (1 inch) cubes. Blanch in boiling salted water for 5 minutes. Drain well.

4 Drain the beans well and place in a bowl. Add the celeriac and toss all the salad ingredients together while the beans and celeriac are still hot. Leave to cool for 20 minutes, then cover and chill for at least 1 hour before serving. Serve chilled.

ORIENTAL SALAD

Serves 8 as a side salad

1 large cucumber
1 small head Chinese leaves
1 red pepper
125 g (4 oz) button mushrooms
225 g (8 oz) beansprouts
30 ml (2 tbsp) soy sauce
15 ml (1 tbsp) peanut butter
30 ml (2 tbsp) sesame oil
30 ml (2 tbsp) rice or wine vinegar
salt and pepper
50 g (2 oz) shelled unsalted peanuts

1 Cut the cucumber in half lengthways. Leave the skin on and scoop out the seeds with a sharp-edged teaspoon and discard. Cut the halves into 5 cm (2 inch) sticks.

2 Shred the Chinese leaves, wash and drain well. Cut the red pepper in half and remove the core and seeds. Cut the flesh into thin strips. Wipe and slice the mushrooms. Rinse the beansprouts and drain well.

3 Just before serving, mix the soy sauce in a large bowl with the peanut butter, oil, vinegar and salt and pepper to taste. Add the salad ingredients and the peanuts and toss together. Transfer to a serving bowl.

Celeriac and Bean Salad

Oriental Salad

GADO-GADO
(Indonesian Mixed Vegetable Salad)

SERVES 4 AS A MAIN MEAL

polyunsaturated oil, for deep-frying
100 g (4 oz) shelled unsalted peanuts
1 small onion, skinned and very finely chopped
2 garlic cloves, skinned and crushed
2.5–5 ml (½–1 tsp) chilli powder
5 ml (1 tsp) raw cane sugar
juice of 1 lemon
25 g (1 oz) creamed coconut, roughly chopped (optional)
8 small waxy new potatoes
4 small young carrots
100 g (4 oz) cauliflower florets
100 g (4 oz) green cabbage or spring greens
100 g (4 oz) French beans
100 g (4 oz) beansprouts
lettuce leaves, cucumber slices and hard-boiled egg, to garnish

1 Make the peanut sauce. Heat the oil to 190°C (375°F) in a wok or deep-fat frier. Lower the peanuts into the hot oil and deep-fry for about 5 minutes until the skins are well browned. Remove with a slotted spoon and drain on absorbent kitchen paper.

2 If using a wok, pour off all but about 30 ml (2 tbsp) of the oil. (If a deep-fat frier was used, pour 30 ml (2 tbsp) of the oil into a heavy-based saucepan.) Reheat the oil, add the onion and garlic and fry for 5 minutes until soft and lightly coloured.

3 Add the chilli powder and stir-fry for 1–2 minutes, then add 350 ml (12 fl oz) water, the sugar, lemon juice and creamed coconut, if using. Bring to the boil, stirring to combine the ingredients.

4 Grind the deep-fried peanuts in a food processor or nut mill, or with a pestle and mortar. Add to the sauce and simmer, stirring, until thickened. Remove and set aside until ready to serve.

5 Scrub the potatoes and carrots. Slice the carrots thinly. Divide the cauliflower into small sprigs. Cut off any thick, hard stalks from the cabbage and discard. Shred the cabbage leaves. Top and tail the French beans.

6 Boil the potatoes in salted water for about 20 minutes until tender. Remove with a slotted spoon and leave until cool enough to handle. Add the carrots to the water and parboil for 4 minutes. Remove with a slotted spoon.

7 Blanch the cauliflower and beans in the water for 3 minutes and remove with a slotted spoon. Blanch the cabbage and beansprouts for 1 minute only, then drain and discard the water. Remove the skin from the potatoes, then slice into thin rings.

8 Line a large shallow serving dish or platter with lettuce leaves. Arrange the vegetables on top, then garnish with the slices of cucumber and hard-boiled egg.

9 Reheat the sauce, stirring constantly, then pour a little over the salad. Serve immediately, with the remaining sauce handed separately in a jug or bowl.

BEETROOT SALAD WITH MINT

SERVES 4–6 AS A SIDE SALAD

120 ml (8 tbsp) chopped fresh mint
700 g (1½ lb) cooked beetroot
150 ml (¼ pint) malt vinegar
5 ml (1 tsp) raw cane sugar
salt and pepper
2 medium onions, skinned and finely sliced into rings

1 Put 90 ml (6 tbsp) of the mint in a bowl and pour over 150 ml (¼ pint) boiling water. Leave to stand for 2–3 minutes.

2 Peel the beetroot and slice thinly. Place in a large shallow dish. Add the vinegar and sugar to the mint and water with salt and pepper to taste. Pour over the beetroot. Cover and chill for 2–3 hours or overnight.

3 To serve, place alternate layers of beetroot and onion in a serving dish. Pour over the mint dressing and garnish with the remaining chopped mint. Serve chilled.

Gado Gado (Indonesian mixed vegetable salad)

BULGAR WHEAT SALAD

SERVES 8 AS A SIDE SALAD

350 g (12 oz) bulgar wheat (cracked wheat)
1 medium cucumber, chopped
175 g (6 oz) walnuts, chopped
60 ml (4 tbsp) chopped fresh dill
90 ml (6 tbsp) polyunsaturated oil
45 ml (3 tbsp) white wine vinegar
1 garlic clove, skinned and crushed
salt and pepper
lettuce leaves and sprigs of dill, to serve

1 Put the bulgar wheat in a bowl, pour in enough cold water to cover and leave to soak for 30 minutes.

2 Squeeze the wheat dry with your hands, then put in a large bowl with the cucumber, walnuts and dill. Mix together well.

3 Put the oil, vinegar, garlic and salt and pepper to taste in a bowl and whisk together until well emulsified.

4 Pour the dressing over the salad and toss well to combine. Pile on to lettuce leaves to serve, and garnish with dill sprigs.

RICE SALAD RING

SERVES 8 AS A SIDE SALAD

225 g (8 oz) long grain brown rice
salt and pepper
1 green pepper, cored, seeded and diced
3 caps canned pimiento, diced
198 g (7 oz) can sweetcorn, drained
75 ml (5 tbsp) chopped fresh parsley
50 g (2 oz) salted peanuts
45 ml (3 tbsp) lemon juice
celery salt
watercress, to garnish

1 Cook the rice in plenty of boiling salted water for 30–35 minutes until tender, then tip into a sieve and drain. Rinse through with hot water from the kettle, then rinse under cold running water and drain thoroughly. Leave to cool completely.

2 Blanch the green pepper in boiling water for 1 minute, drain, then rinse under cold running water and drain again.

3 In a large bowl, mix the cold rice, pepper, pimiento, sweetcorn, parsley, peanuts and lemon juice, and season with celery salt and pepper to taste.

4 Press the salad into a lightly oiled 1.4 litre (2½ pint) ring mould and refrigerate for 1 hour. Turn out on to a flat serving plate and fill with watercress. Serve chilled.

MANGE-TOUT SALAD

SERVES 6 AS A SIDE SALAD

225 g (8 oz) mange-tout, trimmed
salt and pepper
30 ml (2 tbsp) polyunsaturated oil
1 cucumber
30 ml (2 tbsp) single cream
45 ml (3 tbsp) French dressing (see page 155)
chopped fresh parsley and mint

1 Cook the mange-tout in boiling salted water for about 4 minutes; drain and return to the pan. While still hot, add the oil and toss until well coated. Leave to cool for at least 30 minutes, then put in a bowl, cover and chill until required.

2 Cut the cucumber into 5 cm (2 inch) sticks, without peeling. Add to the mange-tout, cover with cling film and chill until required.

3 Whisk the cream and French dressing together with the parsley and mint and pepper to taste. Chill until required.

4 To serve, place the mange-tout and cucumber in a salad bowl. Shake the dressing once more, pour over the vegetables and serve immediately.

CHILLI POTATO SALAD

SERVES 6 AS A SIDE SALAD

900 g (2 lb) even-sized new potatoes
1 medium green pepper
1 medium red pepper
200 ml (7 fl oz) polyunsaturated oil
75 ml (5 tbsp) garlic vinegar
15 ml (1 tbsp) chilli seasoning
salt and pepper
1 medium onion, skinned and chopped
30 ml (2 tbsp) sesame seeds
fresh coriander, to garnish

1 Scrub the potatoes and boil in their skins until tender; about 20 minutes.

Chilli Potato Salad

2 Meanwhile, halve the peppers, then remove the seeds and chop. Blanch them in boiling water for 1–2 minutes. Drain well. In a large bowl, whisk together the oil, vinegar, chilli seasoning and salt and pepper to taste.

3 Drain the potatoes well. Halve them if large, but do not peel them. While still hot, stir into the dressing with the onion and peppers. Cool, cover and chill for about 2 hours.

4 Toast the sesame seeds under the grill, leave to cool, then stir through the salad. Taste and adjust the seasoning before serving, garnished with fresh coriander.

MAYONNAISE

MAKES ABOUT 150 ML (¼ PINT)

1 egg yolk
2.5 ml (½ tsp) mustard powder or 5 ml (1 tsp) Dijon mustard
2.5 ml (½ tsp) salt
1.25 ml (¼ tsp) pepper
2.5 ml (½ tsp) raw cane sugar
15 ml (1 tbsp) white wine vinegar or lemon juice
about 150 ml (¼ pint) polyunsaturated oil

Method I – by hand

1 Put the egg yolk into a bowl with the mustard, salt, pepper, sugar and 5 ml (1 tsp) of the vinegar or lemon juice. Mix thoroughly, then add the oil drop by drop, whisking constantly, until the sauce is thick and smooth. If it becomes too thick, add a little more of the vinegar or lemon juice.

2 When all the oil has been added, add the remaining vinegar or lemon juice gradually and mix thoroughly.

Method II – in a blender or food processor
Most blenders and food processors need at least a two-egg quantity in order to ensure that the blades are covered.

1 Put the yolks, mustard, salt, pepper, sugar and half the vinegar or lemon juice into the blender or food processor and blend well. If your machine has a variable speed control, run it at a slow speed.

2 Add the oil gradually while the machine is running. Add the remaining vinegar and season.

Rescue remedies If the mayonnaise separates, save it by beating the curdled mixture into a fresh base. This base can be any one of the following: 5 ml (1 tsp) hot water; 5 ml (1 tsp) vinegar or lemon juice; 5 ml (1 tsp) Dijon mustard or 2.5 ml (½ tsp) mustard powder; or an egg yolk. Add the curdled mixture to the base, beating hard. When the mixture is smooth, continue adding the oil as above. (If you use an extra egg yolk you may find that you need to add a little extra oil.)
Storing mayonnaise Home-made mayonnaise does not keep as long as bought varieties because it lacks their added emulsifiers, stabilisers and preservatives. However, mayonnaise should keep for 2–3 weeks in the refrigerator. Allow to come to room temperature before stirring or the mayonnaise may curdle.

VARIATIONS

These variations are made by adding the extra ingredients to 150 ml (¼ pint) mayonnaise.

CAPER MAYONNAISE
Add 10 ml (2 tsp) chopped capers, 5 ml (1 tsp) chopped pimiento and 2.5 ml (½ tsp) tarragon vinegar. Caper mayonnaise is ideal for fish.

CUCUMBER MAYONNAISE
Add 30 ml (2 tbsp) finely chopped cucumber and 2.5 ml (½ tsp) salt. This mayonnaise goes well with fish salads, especially crab, lobster and salmon.

BLUE CHEESE DRESSING
Add 150 ml (¼ pint) soured cream, 75 g (3 oz) crumbled blue cheese, 5 ml (1 tsp) vinegar and 1 garlic clove, skinned and crushed, and pepper to taste.

TARTARE SAUCE
Add 5 ml (1 tsp) chopped fresh tarragon or snipped chives, 10 ml (2 tsp) chopped capers, 10 ml (2 tsp) chopped gherkins, 10 ml (2 tsp) chopped fresh parsley and 15 ml (1 tbsp) lemon juice or tarragon vinegar. Leave to stand for at least 1 hour before serving, to allow the flavours to blend.

THOUSAND ISLAND MAYONNAISE
Add 15 ml (1 tbsp) chopped stuffed olives, 5 ml (1 tsp) finely chopped onion, 1 egg, hard-boiled, shelled and chopped, 15 ml (1 tbsp) finely chopped green pepper, 5 ml (1 tsp) chopped fresh parsley and 5 ml (1 tsp) tomato purée.

AÏOLI
(Garlic Mayonnaise)

MAKES 300 ML (½ PINT)

4 garlic cloves, skinned
1.25 ml (¼ tsp) salt
2 egg yolks
300 ml (½ pint) olive oil
30 ml (2 tbsp) lemon juice

1 In a bowl, crush the garlic cloves with a little of the salt to a smooth paste. Add the egg yolks and remaining salt and beat well. Gradually beat in the oil, as for mayonnaise, until thick and smooth.

2 When all the oil has been added, beat in the remaining lemon juice. The dressing can be stored for up to 4 days in a screw-topped jar in the refrigerator.

FRENCH DRESSING
(Sauce Vinaigrette)

MAKES 120 ML (8 TBSP)

90 ml (6 tbsp) polyunsaturated oil
30 ml (2 tbsp) wine or herb vinegar or lemon juice
2.5 ml (½ tsp) raw cane sugar
2.5 ml (½ tsp) mustard, eg wholegrain, Dijon, French, or mustard powder
salt and pepper

1. Put all the ingredients in a bowl or screw-topped jar and whisk or shake until well blended. The dressing separates on standing, so whisk or shake again, if necessary, immediately before use.

2. The dressing can be stored in a bottle or screw-topped jar for a few months in the refrigerator, but shake it vigorously just before serving.

> VARIATIONS
>
> FRESH HERB VINAIGRETTE
> Add 15 ml (1 tbsp) chopped fresh parsley or 15 ml (1 tbsp) chopped fresh mint or 10 ml (2 tsp) snipped fresh chives, or a mixture of all three.
>
> MUSTARD VINAIGRETTE
> Add 15 ml (1 tbsp) wholegrain mustard.
>
> CURRY VINAIGRETTE
> Add 5 ml (1 tsp) curry powder.

PESTO

MAKES 300 ML (½ PINT)

50 g (2 oz) fresh basil leaves
2 garlic cloves, skinned
30 ml (2 tbsp) pine nuts
salt and pepper
50 g (2 oz) freshly grated Parmesan cheese
100 ml (4 fl oz) olive oil
30 ml (2 tbsp) double cream

1. Put the basil, garlic, pine nuts and salt and pepper to taste in a mortar and grind with a pestle until a paste forms. Add the cheese and blend well.

2. Transfer to a bowl and beat in the oil, a little at a time, stirring vigorously with a wooden spoon. This dressing can be stored for up to 2 weeks in a screw-topped jar in the refrigerator.

TOMATO DRESSING

MAKES ABOUT 150 ML (¼ PINT)

30 ml (2 tbsp) tomato juice
30 ml (2 tbsp) cider vinegar
30 ml (2 tbsp) clear honey
1 egg yolk
salt and pepper
30 ml (2 tbsp) chopped fresh chives
parsley sprig
60 ml (4 tbsp) polyunsaturated oil

1. Put the tomato juice, vinegar, honey, egg yolk, salt and pepper to taste, chives and parsley in a blender or food processor and blend for 30 seconds.

2. Gradually add the oil and blend until smooth. Use for crisp mixed vegetable salads.

SOURED CREAM AND WATERCRESS DRESSING

SERVES 4

½ bunch watercress
150 ml (¼ pint) soured cream
2.5 ml (½ tsp) lemon juice
salt and pepper
a little milk

1. Remove and discard the coarse stalks from the watercress, then chop finely. Mix with the soured cream, lemon juice and salt and pepper to taste.

2. Add enough milk to give a pouring consistency. Leave for at least 30 minutes before serving. Use as a dressing for bean salads.

YOGURT DRESSING

MAKES 150 ML (¼ PINT)

150 g (¼ pint) natural yogurt or soured cream
15 ml (1 tbsp) polyunsaturated oil
5–10 ml (1–2 tsp) white wine vinegar
5 ml (1 tsp) wholegrain mustard

Put all the ingredients in a bowl and whisk together until well blended. Chill before serving. The dressing can be stored for up to 1 week in a screw-topped jar in the refrigerator.

BREADS

Bread is one of our staple foods and in a vegetarian diet it is particularly important. Many vegetarian dishes lack essential amino-acids but a mixture of vegetable and grain products, eaten at the same time, can make up for each other's deficiencies. Beans on toast, for example, would together provide all the necessary amino-acids. A wide variety of breads are included here. From Wholemeal Bread to Chappatis, Parathas and Puris from India, Pitta from Greece, Dark Rye Bread and Irish Soda Bread. All are full of flavour and goodness.

WHOLEMEAL BREAD

MAKES TWO 900 G (2 LB) LOAVES

40 g (1½ oz) fresh yeast or 22.5 ml (4½ tsp) dried yeast and 5 ml (1 tsp) raw cane sugar
900 ml (1½ pints) tepid water
1.4 kg (3 lb) strong wholemeal flour
30 ml (2 tbsp) raw cane sugar
20 ml (4 tsp) salt
25 g (1 oz) butter or polyunsaturated margarine

1 Grease two 900 g (2 lb) loaf tins. Blend the fresh yeast with 300 ml (½ pint) of the water. If using dried yeast, sprinkle it into 300 ml (½ pint) water with the sugar and leave in a warm place for 15 minutes, until frothy.

2 Mix together the flour, sugar and salt in a large bowl and rub in the butter or margarine. Stir the yeast liquid into the dry ingredients, adding enough of the remaining water to make a firm dough that leaves the bowl clean.

3 Turn it on to a lightly floured surface and knead for about 10 minutes, until the dough feels firm and elastic and no longer sticky. Shape into a ball, place in a bowl, cover with a clean tea-towel and leave until doubled in size.

4 Turn it on to a floured surface and knead until firm. Divide into two or four pieces and flatten firmly with the knuckles to knock out any air bubbles. Knead again. Shape to fit the tins.

5 Cover with a clean tea-towel and leave to prove until the dough rises almost to the tops of the tins.

6 Bake at 230°C (450°F) mark 8 for 30–40 minutes. Turn out and cool on a wire rack.

A selection of wholemeal bread loaves and rolls

QUICK WHOLEMEAL ROLLS

MAKES 12

15 g (½ oz) fresh yeast or 7.5 ml (1½ tsp) dried
10 ml (2 tsp) raw cane sugar
300 ml (½ pint) tepid water
225 g (8 oz) strong wholemeal flour
225 g (8 oz) strong white flour
10 ml (2 tsp) salt
15 g (½ oz) butter or polyunsaturated margarine
cracked wheat, to decorate

1 Grease a baking sheet. Blend the fresh yeast, 5 ml (1 tsp) of the sugar and the water. If using dried yeast, sprinkle it into the water with 5 ml (1 tsp) of the sugar and leave in a warm place for 15 minutes until frothy.

2 Put the flours into a bowl with the salt and remaining sugar. Rub in the butter or margarine. Add the yeast liquid and mix to a soft dough. Turn on to a lightly floured surface and knead for about 2 minutes until smooth.

3 Divide the dough into 12 equal pieces and shape into rounds. Place on the greased baking sheet, brush with water and sprinkle the tops with cracked wheat. Cover with a clean tea-towel and leave to prove in a warm place for about 1 hour until doubled in size.

4 Bake at 230°C (450°F) mark 8 for 15–20 minutes or until golden brown. Cool for at least 15 minutes on a wire rack.

POPPY SEED GRANARY ROUND

MAKES 8 ROLLS

15 g (½ oz) fresh yeast or 7.5 g (¼ oz) dried yeast and 2.5 ml (½ tsp) raw cane sugar
300 ml (½ pint) tepid water
450 g (1 lb) Granary flour
5 ml (1 tsp) salt
50 g (2 oz) butter or polyunsaturated margarine
50 g (2 oz) Cheddar cheese, grated
25 g (1 oz) poppy seeds

1 Grease a 20.5 cm (8 inch) sandwich tin. Crumble the fresh yeast into the water and stir until dissolved. If using dried yeast, sprinkle it into water mixed with the sugar. Leave in a warm place for 15 minutes until frothy.

2 Make the dough. Put the flour and salt in a large bowl and rub in the butter or margarine. Add the cheese and the poppy seeds, reserving 5 ml (1 tsp) to garnish. Stir in the yeast liquid and mix to a stiff dough.

3 Turn on to a lightly floured surface and knead for 10 minutes until smooth. Place in a bowl, cover with a clean tea-towel and leave to rise in a warm place for about 1 hour until doubled in size.

4 Turn on to a lightly floured surface and knead for 2–3 minutes until smooth. Using a sharp knife, divide the dough into eight equal pieces and shape into neat, even-sized rolls with your hands.

5 Arrange in the tin, cover with a clean tea-towel and leave to prove in a warm place for about 30 minutes until doubled in size.

6 Sprinkle with the reserved poppy seeds. Bake at 200°C (400°F) mark 6 for about 25 minutes until golden brown and sounds hollow when the bottom of the bread is tapped.

DARK RYE BREAD

MAKES 1 LOAF

275 g (10 oz) rye flour
275 g (10 oz) strong white flour
15 g (½ oz) salt
10 ml (2 tsp) caraway or fennel seeds
150 ml (¼ pint) tepid water
150 ml (¼ pint) tepid milk
15 ml (1 tbsp) black treacle
25 g (1 oz) fresh yeast or 15 ml (1 tbsp) dried yeast and 5 ml (1 tsp) raw cane sugar

1 Grease two baking sheets. Mix together the flours and salt in a bowl. Stir in the caraway or fennel seeds.

2 Combine the water, milk and treacle, crumble in the fresh yeast and stir until blended. If using dried yeast, sprinkle it into the water and milk with the sugar and leave in a warm place for 15 minutes, until the yeast is frothy.

3 Pour the liquid into the flour mixture and mix to a firm dough, adding extra flour if required. Turn the dough on to a lightly floured surface and knead for about 10 minutes, until the dough feels firm and elastic and no longer sticky.

4 Place in a bowl, cover with a clean tea-towel and leave to rise until doubled in size. Turn the dough on to a lightly floured surface, knead well and divide into two. Shape into traditional cobs by kneading into a ball until the underside is smooth.

5 Turn it over and place on the greased baking sheets and cover with a clean tea-towel. Leave to prove until doubled in size and the dough springs back when lightly pressed with a floured finger.

6 Bake at 190°C (375°F) mark 5 for 30 minutes. Brush the tops with water, reduce the oven temperature to 180°C (350°F) mark 4 and bake for 20 minutes more. Cool on a wire rack.

CHEESE SCONES

MAKES ABOUT 20

450 g (1 lb) plain wholemeal flour
5 ml (1 tsp) salt
5 ml (1 tsp) bicarbonate of soda
50 g (2 oz) butter or polyunsaturated margarine
100 g (4 oz) Cheddar cheese, grated
10 ml (2 tsp) vegetable yeast extract
150 ml (¼ pint) boiling water
150 ml (¼ pint) natural yogurt

1 Put the flour into a bowl with the salt and bicarbonate of soda. Rub in the butter or margarine until the mixture resembles fine crumbs. Stir in the cheese. Dissolve the yeast extract in the boiling water and leave to cool slightly.

2 Make a well in the centre of the flour mixture and pour in the dissolved yeast extract and the yogurt. Mix to a soft dough. Turn on to a floured surface and knead until smooth. Roll out to about 1.5 cm (¾ inch) thick and cut into rounds using a 5 cm (2 inch) cutter.

3 Put on a floured baking sheet and bake at 200°C (400°F) mark 6 for 20 minutes until well risen and brown. Eat the scones hot or leave them to cool on a wire rack.

SODA BREAD

MAKES 1 LOAF

225 g (8 oz) plain wholemeal flour
225 g (8 oz) plain white flour
10 ml (2 tsp) bicarbonate of soda
10 ml (2 tsp) cream of tartar
5 ml (1 tsp) salt
25 g (1 oz) butter or polyunsaturated margarine
about 300 ml (½ pint) buttermilk

1 Grease and flour a baking sheet. Sift together the dry ingredients twice. Stir in the bran (from the wholemeal flour) left in the bottom of the sieve. Rub in the butter or margarine. Mix to a soft dough with the buttermilk, adding a little at a time.

2 Shape into an 18 cm (7 inch) round and mark into triangles. Put on the baking sheet and bake at 220°C (425°F) mark 7 for about 30 minutes. Eat while very fresh.

CHAPPATIS
(Unleavened Wholemeal Bread)

MAKES 8–10

225 g (8 oz) plain wholemeal flour
melted ghee or polyunsaturated margarine, for brushing

1 Put the flour in a bowl and gradually mix in 150–200 ml (5–7 fl oz) water to form a stiff dough.

2 Turn on to a lightly floured surface and, with floured hands, knead thoroughly for 6–8 minutes until smooth and elastic. Return the dough to the bowl, cover with a clean damp tea-towel and leave to rest for 15 minutes.

3 Heat a tava (flat Indian frying pan), a heavy frying pan or griddle over a low heat. Divide the dough into 8–10 pieces. With floured hands, take a piece of dough and shape into a smooth ball. Dip in flour to coat, then put on to a floured surface and roll out to a round about 12.5 cm (5 inches) in diameter and 0.25 cm (½ inch) thick.

4 Slap the chappati on to the hot pan or griddle. As soon as brown specks appear on the underside, turn it over and repeat on the other side. Turn it over again and, with a clean tea-towel, press down the edges of the chappati to circulate the steam and make the chappati puff up. Cook until the underside is golden brown, then cook the other side in the same way.

5 Brush with melted ghee or margarine. Serve at once or keep warm wrapped in foil. Cook the remaining chappatis in the same way.

PITTA BREAD

MAKES 6

450 g (1 lb) plain wholemeal flour
7.5 ml (1½ tsp) baking powder
5 ml (1 tsp) salt
1 egg, beaten
30 ml (2 tbsp) polyunsaturated oil
225 ml (8 fl oz) natural yogurt
about 100 ml (4 fl oz) milk

1 Sift the flour, baking powder and salt into a bowl. Stir in the bran left in the bottom of the sieve. Make a well in the centre and stir in the egg, oil, yogurt and enough of the milk to form a soft dough.

2 Turn on to a lightly floured surface and knead well for 2–3 minutes until smooth. Divide into 6 equal pieces and roll out each piece into an oval shape about 20.5 cm (8 inch) long.

3 Preheat a grill. Place 2 pitta breads on a baking sheet and brush each with a little water. Grill under a moderate heat for 2–3 minutes on each side until golden brown. Serve while still warm.

PURIS
(Deep-Fried Unleavened Wholemeal Bread)

MAKES 12

225 g (8 oz) plain wholemeal flour
salt
30 ml (2 tbsp) polyunsaturated oil or melted ghee
polyunsaturated oil, for deep frying

1 Put the flour and a pinch of salt in a bowl. Sprinkle the oil or melted ghee over the top. Gradually mix in 150–200 ml (5–7 fl oz) water to form a stiff dough. Turn on to a lightly floured surface and knead thoroughly for 6–8 minutes until smooth and elastic. Cover with a clean damp tea-towel and leave to rest for 15 minutes.

2 Divide the dough into 12 and roll each piece into a small ball. On a lightly floured surface, roll out one ball to a round about 12.5 cm (5 inches) in diameter, keeping the others covered. If you have the space, roll out the remaining puris in the same way and, as you proceed, cover with a damp tea-towel.

3 Heat about 5 cm (2 inches) of oil in a small, deep frying pan until very hot. Carefully slide a puri into the hot fat. Using the back of a slotted spoon, press the puri into the oil and cook for about 10 seconds. It will begin to puff up immediately. Turn the puri over and, still pressing with the spoon, fry until golden brown and puffed up.

4 Drain the puri on absorbent kitchen paper and serve hot. Cook the remaining puris in the same way.

PARATHAS
(Shallow-Fried Unleavened Wholemeal Bread)

MAKES 8

225 g (8 oz) plain wholemeal flour
melted ghee or polyunsaturated margarine, for brushing

1 Put the flour in a bowl and gradually mix in 150–200 ml (5–7 fl oz) water to form a stiff dough. Turn on to a lightly floured surface and, with floured hands, knead thoroughly for 6–8 minutes until smooth and elastic.

2 Return the dough to the bowl, cover with a clean damp tea-towel and leave to rest for 15 minutes.

3 Divide the dough into 8 pieces. With floured hands, take a piece of dough and shape into a smooth ball. Dip in flour to coat, then roll out on a floured surface to a round about 15 cm (6 inches) in diameter. Brush a little melted ghee or margarine on top. Roll the round into a tube shape, hold the tube upright and place one end in the centre of your hand. Carefully wind the rest of the roll around the centre point to form a disc. Press lightly together and using a little extra flour, roll out thinly into a round about 15 cm (6 inches) in diameter.

4 Cover with a damp tea-towel and roll out the remaining dough to make 8 parathas.

5 Heat a tava (flat Indian frying pan), a heavy frying pan or griddle over a low heat. Put one of the parathas on to the hot pan or griddle and cook until small bubbles appear on the surface. Turn it over and brush the top with melted ghee or margarine. Cook until the underside is golden brown, turn again and brush with ghee or margarine. Press down the edges with a spatula to ensure even cooking and cook the other side until golden brown.

6 Brush with ghee or margarine and serve at once or keep warm wrapped in foil. Cook the remaining parathas in the same way.

SPINACH STUFFED PARATHAS

MAKES 12

450 g (1 lb) plain wholemeal flour
salt
125 g (4 oz) unsalted cashew nuts
75 g (3 oz) ghee or 90 ml (6 tbsp) polyunsaturated oil
2.5 ml (½ tsp) chilli powder
5 ml (1 tsp) cumin seeds
228 g (8 oz) frozen spinach, thawed and drained

1 Put the flour and a pinch of salt in a mixing bowl. Bind to a soft dough with about 350 ml (1 fl oz) water. Turn on to a lightly floured surface nd knead for 6–8 minutes until smooth and elastic. Cover with a damp tea-towel and leave to rest for about 15 minutes.

2 Meanwhile, chop the nuts quite finely. Heat 25 g (1 oz) ghee or 30 ml (2 tbsp) oil in a small frying pan. Add the nuts and chilli powder and fry gently for 2–3 minutes, stirring frequently, until the nuts just begin to colour.

3 Remove the pan from the heat and stir in the cumin seeds and a little salt. Turn out into a bowl, leave to cool slightly, then stir in the spinach.

4 Divide the dough into twelve pieces. Roll each one out to a round about 10 cm (4 inches) in diameter. Spoon the filling into the centre of each and fold over the dough to completely enclose the filling. Press the edges well together to seal.

5 On a well floured surface and using a floured rolling pin, roll out each filled dough round to a 12.5–15 cm (5–6 inch) circle. Melt the remaining ghee or oil in a small saucepan, then set aside.

6 Heat a tava (flat Indian frying pan), small heavy frying pan or griddle. Put one paratha on to the pan or griddle and cook over a moderate heat for about 1 minute until beginning to brown. Turn over and cook the second side in the same way. Smear a little of the melted ghee or oil over the top of the paratha. Turn over and fry the oily side for about 30 seconds or until well browned, pressing down the edges to ensure even cooking. Smear ghee or oil over the top of the paratha, turn over and fry the second side until well browned. Remove from the pan.

7 Serve at once or keep warm wrapped in foil. Cook the remaining parathas in the same way.

PUDDINGS, CAKES AND BISCUITS

In a vegetarian diet, most puddings, cakes and biscuits can be included. Nevertheless, many vegetarians are health-conscious and want to eat an overall healthy diet. Fresh and dried fruits are a natural choice but there are occasions when you want a change. For this reason I have included a selection of recipes. Enjoy them but eat in moderation! Spiced Apple and Plum Crumble, for example, uses natural, wholefood ingredients as does Crunchy Pears in Cinnamon and Honey Wine. Banana Whips, too, are a healthy wholefood dessert that particularly appeals to children. Cream Crowdie on the other hand is rich and creamy, as is Tangerine Syllabub. Serve them for a special dinner party when you wish to be indulgent. For a tea-time treat why not make a Carrot Cake, Apple Cake or a batch of Apricot Crunches – all are full of wholefood nourishment.

PINEAPPLE AND BANANA FLAMBÉ

SERVES 6–8

1 medium pineapple
900 g (2 lb) firm bananas
125 g (4 oz) dried figs
50 g (2 oz) butter or polyunsaturated margarine
125 g (4 oz) raw cane demerara sugar
45 ml (3 tbsp) lemon juice
2.5 ml (½ tsp) ground mixed spice
60 ml (4 tbsp) dark rum

1 Cut the pineapple into 1 cm (½ inch) slices. Snip off the skin and cut the flesh into chunks, discarding the core.

2 Peel and thickly slice the bananas into the bottom of a shallow ovenproof dish; spoon the pineapple on top.

3 Cut the figs into coarse shreds and scatter over the fruit. Put the butter or margarine, sugar, strained lemon juice and spice together in a saucepan and heat until well blended. Pour over the prepared fruit.

4 Cover tightly and bake at 200°C (400°F) mark 6 for 25 minutes until the fruit is tender.

5 Heat the rum gently in a small saucepan, remove from the heat and ignite with a match. Pour immediately over the fruit and bring the dish to the table while still flaming.

Pineapple and Banana Flambé

ICED ORANGE SABAYON

SERVES 6

6 egg yolks
175 g (6 oz) raw cane demerara sugar
90 ml (6 tbsp) orange-flavoured liqueur
200 ml (7 fl oz) unsweetened orange juice
glacé cherries and candied peel, to decorate

1 Put the egg yolks and sugar in a bowl and beat together until pale and creamy. Stir in the liqueur and orange juice.

2 Pour into a medium heavy-based saucepan. Stir over low heat until the mixture thickens and just coats the back of the spoon. Do *not* boil.

3 Pour into 6 individual soufflé dishes or ramekins and cool for at least 30 minutes. Freeze for 3–4 hours until firm. Wrap in cling film and return to the freezer.

4 Serve straight from the freezer, decorated with glacé cherries and candied peel.

Iced Orange Sabayon

BANANA WHIPS

Serves 4

2 egg whites
300 ml (½ pint) natural set yogurt
finely grated rind and juice of ½ orange
60 ml (4 tbsp) raw cane sugar
2 medium bananas
50 g (2 oz) crunchy breakfast cereal

1. Whisk the egg whites until stiff. Put the yogurt in a bowl and stir until smooth. Fold in the egg whites until evenly incorporated.

2. In a separate bowl, mix together the orange rind and juice and the sugar. Peel the bananas and slice thinly into the juice mixture. Fold gently to mix.

3. Put a layer of the yogurt mixture in the bottom of 4 individual glasses. Cover with a layer of cereal, then with a layer of the banana mixture. Repeat these 3 layers once more. Serve immediately.

Banana Whips

SPICED APPLE AND PLUM CRUMBLE

SERVES 6

450 g (1 lb) plums
700 g (1½ lb) cooking apples
100 g (4 oz) butter or polyunsaturated margarine
100 g (4 oz) raw cane sugar
7.5 ml (1½ tsp) ground mixed spice
175 g (6 oz) plain wholemeal flour
50 g (2 oz) blanched hazelnuts, toasted and chopped

1 Using a sharp knife, cut the plums in half and remove the stones. Peel, quarter, core and slice the apples and put in a medium saucepan with 25 g (1 oz) of the butter or margarine, half the sugar and about 5 ml (1 tsp) mixed spice.

2 Cover the pan and cook gently for 15 minutes until the apples begin to soften. Stir in the plums and turn into a 1.1 litre (2 pint) shallow ovenproof dish. Leave to cool for about 30 minutes.

3 Stir the flour and remaining mixed spice well together, then rub in the remaining butter or margarine until the mixture resembles fine crumbs. Stir in the rest of the sugar with the hazelnuts.

4 Spoon the crumble mixture over the fruit and bake at 180°C (350°F) mark 4 for about 40 minutes or until the top is golden, crisp and crumbly.

Spiced Apple and Plum Crumble

POACHED PEARS IN GINGER SYRUP

SERVES 4

150 ml (¼ pint) dry white wine
75 ml (5 tbsp) ginger wine
75 g (3 oz) raw cane sugar
1 strip of lemon rind
1 cinnamon stick
4 firm pears
30 ml (2 tbsp) preserved ginger in syrup, thinly sliced
pouring cream, to serve

1 Pour the white wine into a large heavy-base saucepan. Add 300 ml (½ pint) water, the ginger wine, sugar, lemon rind and cinnamon stick. Heat gently until the sugar has dissolved, then remove from the heat.

2 Using a vegetable peeler or cannelle knife, peel the pears from top to bottom in a spiral pattern. Leave the stalks on. Put the pears in the wine and simmer gently for 30 minutes. Transfer to a serving bowl.

3 Boil the liquid in the pan until reduced by half, then strain and stir in the preserved ginger. Pour over the pears in the bowl.

4 Leave the pears for 1–2 hours until completely cold, spooning the syrup over them occasionally, then chill overnight. Serve chilled, with pouring cream.

CRUNCHY PEARS IN CINNAMON AND HONEY WINE

SERVES 4–6

60 ml (4 tbsp) white wine, vermouth or sherry
60 ml (4 tbsp) clear honey
5 ml (1 tsp) ground cinnamon
50 g (2 oz) butter or polyunsaturated margarine
100 g (4 oz) wholemeal breadcrumbs (made from a day-old loaf)
50 g (2 oz) raw cane demerara sugar
4 ripe dessert pears

1 In a jug, mix together the wine, honey and half of the cinnamon. Set aside.

2 Melt the butter or margarine in a small pan, add the breadcrumbs, sugar and remaining cinnamon and stir together until evenly mixed. Set aside.

3 Peel and halve the pears, removing the cores. Arrange the pear halves, cut side down, in a greased ovenproof dish and pour over the white wine mixture.

4 Sprinkle the pears evenly with the breadcrumb mixture and bake at 190°C (375°F) mark 5 for 40 minutes. Serve hot, accompanied by yogurt flavoured with grated orange rind, if liked.

CREAM CROWDIE

SERVES 4

50 g (2 oz) medium oatmeal
300 ml (½ pint) double cream
60 ml (4 tbsp) clear honey
45 ml (3 tbsp) whisky
350 g (12 oz) fresh raspberries, hulled

1 Place the oatmeal in a grill pan (without the rack) and toast until golden brown, turning occasionally with a spoon. Leave for 15 minutes until cool.

2 Whip the cream until just standing in soft peaks, then stir in the honey, whisky and cooled toasted oatmeal.

3 Reserve a few raspberries for decoration, then layer up the remaining raspberries and fresh cream mixture in four tall glasses. Cover with cling film and refrigerate for at least 1 hour.

4 Allow to come to room temperature for 30 minutes before serving. Decorate each glass with the reserved raspberries.

Cream Crowdie

Crunchy Pears in Cinnamon and Honey Wine

DANISH 'PEASANT GIRL IN A VEIL'

SERVES 4

50 g (2 oz) butter or polyunsaturated margarine
175 g (6 oz) fresh wholemeal breadcrumbs
75 g (3 oz) raw cane sugar
700 g (1½ lb) cooking apples
juice of ½ a lemon
raw cane sugar
150 ml (¼ pint) double or whipping cream
50 g (2 oz) grated chocolate or carob, to decorate

1 Melt the butter or margarine in a frying pan. Mix the crumbs and sugar together and fry in the hot fat until crisp, stirring frequently with a wooden spoon to prevent the crumbs from catching and burning.

2 Peel, core and slice the apples. Put them in a saucepan with 30 ml (2 tbsp) water, the lemon juice and some sugar to taste. Cover and cook gently for 10–15 minutes until they form a pulp. Leave to cool, then taste for sweetness.

3 Put alternate layers of the fried crumb mixture and the apple pulp into a glass dish, finishing with a layer of crumbs. Refrigerate for 2–3 hours.

4 Whip the cream until stiff. Pipe over the top of the crumb mixture and decorate with grated chocolate. Serve chilled.

Danish 'Peasant Girl in a Veil'

Individual Chocolate Mousses

INDIVIDUAL CHOCOLATE MOUSSES

SERVES 6

350 g (12 oz) plain chocolate
6 eggs, separated
30 ml (2 tbsp) rum or brandy
150 ml (¼ pint) double cream
chocolate curls, to decorate

1 Break the chocolate into a heatproof bowl. Put the bowl over a pan of simmering water and heat until melted, stirring occasionally.

2 Remove from the heat and beat in the egg yolks and rum. Whisk the egg whites until stiff, then fold into the chocolate mixture. Spoon into six ramekin dishes and chill for 2–3 hours until set.

3 Whip the cream until stiff. Decorate the mousses with piped cream and chocolate curls.

TANGERINE SYLLABUB

SERVES 6

700 g (1½ lb) tangerines – about 6
30 ml (2 tbsp) lemon juice
30 ml (2 tbsp) orange-flavoured liqueur
50 g (2 oz) raw cane sugar
300 ml (½ pint) double cream
sponge fingers, to serve

1 Finely grate the rind from 3 tangerines into a small bowl; use a stiff brush to remove all the rind from the teeth of the grater. Peel these 3 tangerines and pull the segments apart, removing any tough membranes.

2 Halve and squeeze the remaining tangerines. Measure out 120 ml (8 tbsp) juice and strain over the tangerine rinds. Add the lemon juice and liqueur, cover and leave to soak for at least 2 hours.

3 Put the sugar in a bowl and strain in the liquid. Mix well until the sugar has dissolved. Whip the cream until stiff, then gradually whisk in the juices, keeping the cream thick.

4 Put the tangerine segments in the base of 6 stemmed glasses, reserving 6 segments for decoration. Divide the cream mixture between the glasses, cover with cling film and chill for 2 hours.

5 Decorate with tangerine segments and serve with sponge fingers.

Carob and Nut Cake

CAROB AND NUT CAKE

Serves 6–8

175 g (6 oz) butter or polyunsaturated margarine
100 g (4 oz) raw cane sugar
4 eggs, separated
75 g (3 oz) plain wholemeal flour
25 g (1 oz) carob powder
pinch of salt
finely grated rind and juice of 1 orange
two 75 g (2.65 oz) orange-flavoured or plain carob bars
75 g (3 oz) shelled walnuts, chopped

1 Grease and base-line two 18 cm (7 inch) sandwich tins. Put 125 g (4 oz) of the butter or margarine in a bowl with the sugar and beat until light and fluffy. Beat in the egg yolks one at a time.

2 Sift together the flour, carob powder and salt, stirring in any bran left in the sieve. Fold into the creamed mixture with the orange rind and 15 ml (1 tbsp) of the orange juice.

3 Whisk the egg whites until stiff, then fold into the cake mixture until evenly incorporated. Divide the mixture equally between the prepared tins and level the surfaces. Bake at 180°C (350°F) mark 4 for 20 minutes or until risen and firm to the touch.

4 Leave to cool for 1–2 minutes, turn out on to a wire rack and peel off the lining papers. Turn the cakes the right way up and leave to cool completely.

5 Pour the remaining orange juice into a bowl over a pan of simmering water. Break the carob bars into the juice and stir until melted. Remove from heat and beat in remaining butter or margarine. Cool for 10 minutes, stirring occasionally.

6 Spread half the carob mixture over 1 cake and sprinkle with half the walnuts. Top with the other cake and swirl the remaining melted carob over. Sprinkle remaining nuts around the edge.

Note

Carob is produced from the carob bean and is naturally sweet. It contains vitamins A and D, some B vitamins and minerals calcium and magnesium, also protein and a small amount of fibre. Carob powder contains less fat and sodium than cocoa and no caffeine. Carob powder and bars are obtainable from health food shops.

FLAPJACKS

MAKES 8–10

75 g (3 oz) butter or polyunsaturated margarine
50 g (2 oz) raw cane sugar
30 ml (2 tbsp) honey
175 g (6 oz) rolled oats

1 Grease a shallow 18 cm (7 inch) square cake tin. Melt the butter or margarine with the sugar and honey and pour on to the rolled oats. Mix well, turn into the prepared tin and press down well.

2 Bake at 180°C (350°F) mark 4 for about 20 minutes, until golden brown. Cool slightly in the tin, mark into fingers with a sharp knife and loosen round the edges.

3 When firm, remove from the tin and cool on a wire rack, then break into fingers. The flapjacks may be stored in an airtight container for up to a week.

MIXED FRUIT TEABREAD

SERVES 8–10

175 g (6 oz) raisins
125 g (4 oz) sultanas
50 g (2 oz) currants
175 g (6 oz) raw cane sugar
300 ml (½ pint) strained cold tea
1 egg, beaten
225 g (8 oz) plain wholemeal flour
7.5 ml (1½ tsp) baking powder
2.5 ml (½ tsp) ground mixed spice

1 Put the fruit and sugar in a bowl. Pour over the tea, stir well and leave overnight.

2 The next day, add the egg, flour, baking powder and mixed spice to the fruit and tea mixture. Beat thoroughly with a wooden spoon until all the ingredients are evenly combined.

3 Spoon the mixture into a greased and base-lined 900 g (2 lb) loaf tin. Level the surface. Bake at 180°C (350°F) mark 4 for 1¼ hours until risen and a skewer inserted in the centre comes out clean.

4 Turn the cake out of the tin and leave on a wire rack until completely cold. Wrap in cling film and store in an airtight container for 1–2 days before slicing and eating.

Mixed Fruit Teabread

PANCAKES CREOLE

SERVES 4–6

pancake batter made with 300 ml (½ pint) milk (see page 184)
finely grated rind and juice of 1 lime
50 g (2 oz) butter or polyunsaturated margarine
50 g (2 oz) raw cane demerara sugar
60 ml (4 tbsp) dark rum
2.5 ml (½ tsp) ground cinnamon
3–4 bananas
orange and lime twists, to decorate

1 Make 8–12 pancakes in the usual way (see page 184). Slide each pancake out of the pan on to a warm plate and stack with greaseproof paper in between.

2 Put the lime rind and juice in a saucepan with the butter or margarine, sugar, rum and cinnamon. Heat gently until the fat has melted and the sugar dissolved, stirring occasionally.

3 Peel the bananas and slice thinly into the sauce. Cook gently for 5 minutes until tender.

4 Remove the banana slices from the sauce with a slotted spoon. Put a few slices in the centre of each pancake, then fold the pancakes into 'envelopes' around the cooked bananas.

5 Place in a warmed serving dish and pour over the hot sauce. Decorate with orange and lime twists and serve with cream, if liked.

APPLE CAKE

SERVES 8

225 g (8 oz) wholemeal flour
10 ml (2 tsp) freshly grated nutmeg
5 ml (1 tsp) ground cinnamon
10 ml (2 tsp) baking powder
225 g (8 oz) cooking apples, peeled, cored and chopped
125 g (4 oz) butter or polyunsaturated margarine
225 g (8 oz) raw cane sugar
2 eggs, beaten
a little milk (optional)
15 ml (1 tbsp) clear honey
15 ml (1 tbsp) raw cane demerara sugar

1 Grease an 18 cm (7 inch) deep round cake tin. Line with greaseproof paper and grease the paper.

2 Put the wholemeal flour, nutmeg, cinnamon and baking powder into a bowl. Mix in the cooking apples.

3 In a mixing bowl, beat the butter or margarine and sugar until pale and fluffy. Add the eggs, a little at a time, and continue to beat.

4 Fold the flour mixture into the creamed mixture to give a dropping consistency, adding a little milk if necessary.

5 Turn the mixture into the tin and bake at 170°C (325°F) mark 3 for about 1½ hours. Turn out on to a wire rack to cool for 1–2 hours. Brush with honey and sprinkle with the demerara sugar to decorate. Eat within 1–2 days.

CARROT CAKE

SERVES 8

225 g (8 oz) self raising wholemeal flour
5 ml (1 tsp) baking powder
225 g (8 oz) raw cane sugar
225 ml (8 fl oz) polyunsaturated oil
4 eggs, beaten
350 g (12 oz) carrots, peeled and coarsely grated
finely grated rind and juice of 1 lemon
100 g (4 oz) walnut pieces, chopped
175 g (6 oz) Quark
10 ml (2 tsp) clear honey
8 walnut halves, to decorate

1 Grease and base-line a 20.5 (8 inch) round cake tin. Put the flour, baking powder and sugar into a bowl. Add the oil, eggs, carrots, lemon rind, lemon juice and the walnuts and beat together until well mixed. Spoon the mixture into the tin and level the surface.

2 Bake at 180°C (350°F) mark 4 for about 1½ hours until well risen and golden brown. Cover lightly with a piece of greaseproof paper, if necessary to prevent over-browning. Turn out and cool on a wire rack.

3 Make the icing by beating together the Quark and honey. Spoon the mixture on to the top of the cake and using a palette knife spread evenly over the surface. Decorate with the walnut halves.

APRICOT CRUNCH

MAKES 16 WEDGES

75 g (3 oz) dried apricots
100 g (4 oz) butter or polyunsaturated margarine
100 g (4 oz) raw cane demerara sugar
75 ml (5 tbsp) clear honey
200 g (7 oz) crunchy toasted muesli cereal
140 g (5 oz) rolled oats
2.5 ml (½ tsp) mixed spice
10 ml (2 tsp) lemon juice

1. Grease two 18 cm (7 inch) round sandwich tins. Line with greaseproof paper and grease the paper.

2. Simmer the apricots gently in 200 ml (7 fl oz) water for about 10 minutes, or until softened. Blend the contents of the saucepan in a blender or food processor to form a smooth purée. Cool for about 1 hour.

3. In a pan, slowly melt the butter or margarine, sugar and honey. Stir in the cereal and oats and continue stirring until thoroughly combined. Add the puréed apricots, mixed spice and lemon juice. Mix well.

4. Divide the mixture between the prepared tins and spread evenly over the base. Press down well to level the surface.

5. Bake at 180°C (350°F) mark 4 for about 35 minutes. Cut each round into eight wedges. Cool in the tin for 30 minutes until firm. Carefully ease the wedges out of the tin and store in an airtight container when completely cold.

Apricot Crunch

Drinks

Drinks are often forgotten as food. There is always milk but why not try Orange Refresher or Hawaiian Quencher. Both are a meal in a glass and a delicious and time-saving way of keeping your energy level high, especially during hot summer days. Yogurt and Fruity Vitality Drinks make a quick nourishing breakfast. Simply whizz them up in a blender. For drinks that are high in vitamins and minerals try Iced Carrot and Orange Juice – based on raw vegetables and fruit. In order that the drinks can be digested slowly, serve them with straws.

YOGURT VITALITY DRINK

SERVES 1

1 small banana
10 ml (2 tsp) wheatgerm
juice of 1 orange
150 ml (1/4 pint) natural yogurt
1 egg yolk

Peel the banana and slice into a blender or food processor. Add remaining ingredients and blend to a smooth mixture. Pour into a tall glass and serve immediately.

FRUITY VITALITY DRINK

SERVES 1

2 pink grapefruit
1 lemon
1 egg
10 ml (2 tsp) honey, or to taste
5 ml (1 tsp) wheatgerm

1 Squeeze the juice from the grapefruit and lemon, and pour into a blender or food processor.

2 Add the egg, honey and wheatgerm and blend until well combined. Taste for sweetness and add more honey, if liked. Pour into a tall glass and serve immediately.

***left to right:* Fruity Vitality Drink, Vegetable Vitality Drink (see page 180), Yogurt Vitality Drink**

VEGETABLE VITALITY DRINK

SERVES 1

50 g (2 oz) shredded coconut
300 ml (½ pint) boiling water
225 g (8 oz) carrots
juice of ½ lemon
5 ml (1 tsp) wheatgerm oil

1 Put the coconut in a heatproof jug, pour on the boiling water and stir well to mix. Leave to infuse for 30 minutes.

2 Meanwhile, scrub the carrots with a stiff vegetable brush to remove any soil from their skins. Grate into a blender or food processor, add the lemon juice and work until the carrots are broken down to a pulp.

3 Strain the carrot pulp through a sieve into a jug, then strain in the milk from the coconut. Add the wheatgerm oil and whisk vigorously to combine. Pour into a tall glass and serve immediately.

TOMATO AND YOGURT COCKTAIL

SERVES 2

4 tomatoes
150 ml (¼ pint) natural yogurt
Tabasco sauce
lemon juice
paprika
salt
fresh mint sprigs, to garnish

1 Chop the tomatoes roughly, then purée in a blender or food processor. Press the purée through a sieve into a bowl.

2 Whisk in the yogurt, then season to taste with Tabasco sauce, lemon juice, paprika and salt.

3 Pour into tall glasses and float a sprig of mint on top of each to garnish.

FRESH TOMATO JUICE

MAKES 450 ML (¾ PINT)

900 g (2 lb) ripe tomatoes
Tabasco sauce
lemon juice
salt and pepper

1 Chop the tomatoes roughly, then work in a blender or food processor until puréed. Press the tomato purée through a sieve into a bowl.

2 Season to taste with Tabasco sauce, lemon juice and salt and pepper. Pour into a jug or individual glasses. Chill before serving.

HONEY AND YOGURT COOLER

SERVES 1

1 egg
15 ml (1 tbsp) clear honey
300 ml (½ pint) natural yogurt
juice of 1 orange

Put all the ingredients into a blender or food processor and blend for 1 minute. Pour into a tall glass and serve immediately.

ICED CARROT AND ORANGE JUICE

MAKES 900 ML (1½ PINTS)

450 g (1 lb) carrots, peeled
600 ml (1 pint) fresh orange juice
soda water

1 Slice the carrots, put in a saucepan and pour in enough orange juice to cover. Cover the pan, bring to the boil and simmer for about 20 minutes or until the carrots are tender.

2 Put the carrots with their cooking liquid in a blender or food processor and blend until smooth. Allow to cool completely, then chill.

3 Add the remaining orange juice, pour into tall glasses and top up with soda water to taste.

NUTTY BANANA WHIRL

SERVES 2

568 ml (1 pint) chilled milk
1 banana, peeled and thinly sliced
5 ml (1 tsp) clear honey
a few drops of lemon juice
50 g (2 oz) almonds, chopped

Put all the ingredients into a blender or food processor and blend for about 1 minute until frothy. Pour into tall glasses and serve immediately.

ORANGE REFRESHER

SERVES 1

150 ml (¼ pint) natural yogurt
150 ml (¼ pint) fresh orange juice
slice of orange

In a blender, food processor or bowl, whisk the yogurt and orange juice together. Pour into a serving glass and add a slice of orange.

HAWAIIAN QUENCHER

SERVES 2

150 ml (¼ pint) natural yogurt
150 ml (¼ pint) pineapple juice
5 ml (1 tsp) clear honey
fresh pineapple, cubed

Whisk the yogurt, pineapple juice and honey together until blended. Serve in tumblers with pineapple cubes.

BASIC RECIPES

Several basic recipes are needed again and again to make the dishes in this book, so to avoid repetition I have collected them together in this chapter for easy reference. You will find pastry, pasta, pizza, pancakes, stock, sauces, rice and bread accompaniments.

WHOLEMEAL PASTRY

WHEN A RECIPE REQUIRES 175 G (6 OZ) PASTRY, THIS REFERS TO THE WEIGHT OF FLOUR. FOR ANY QUANTITY OF WHOLEMEAL PASTRY, USE HALF FAT TO FLOUR.

175 g (6 oz) plain wholemeal flour
pinch of salt
75 g (3 oz) butter or polyunsaturated margarine or 60 ml (4 tbsp) polyunsaturated oil

1. Mix the flour and salt together in a bowl and add the butter or margarine in small pieces. Using both hands, rub the butter or margarine into the flour between finger and thumb tips until the mixture resembles fine crumbs. If using oil, sprinkle into the flour and mix in with a fork.

2. Add 60 ml (4 tbsp) water all at once, sprinkling it evenly over the surface. Stir the water in with a round-bladed knife until the mixture begins to stick together in large lumps. Add more water if necessary.

3. With one hand, collect the mixture together and knead lightly for a few seconds, to give a firm smooth dough. The pastry can be used straight away, but is better allowed to 'rest' for 15 minutes. It can also be wrapped in polythene and kept in the refrigerator for 1–2 days.

4. When the pastry is required, sprinkle a very little flour on the working surface and on the rolling pin, not on the pastry, and roll out the dough evenly in one direction only, turning occasionally. The usual thickness is about 0.3 cm (⅛ inch). Do not pull or stretch the dough. Use as required. The usual oven temperature for wholemeal pastry is 200–220°C (400–425°F) mark 6–7.

Wholemeal Pastry, used here to line a mincemeat tart

WHOLEMEAL PASTA

SERVES 3–4

175 g (6 oz) plain wholemeal flour
1 egg
1 egg white
30 ml (2 tbsp) olive oil
5 ml (1 tsp) salt

1 Place the flour in a large bowl. Make a well in the centre and add the egg, egg white, oil, salt and 15 ml (1 tbsp) water. Mix together to form a soft dough.

2 Knead the dough for 10 minutes on a lightly floured surface until smooth and elastic. Re-flour the surface and roll out the dough to form a large paper-thin rectangle of pasta.

3 Lay the pasta on a clean dry tea-towel. Let one third of the pasta sheet hang over the side of the table and turn it every 10 minutes to help dry the pasta more quickly. This process takes about 30 minutes: the pasta is ready when it is dry and looks leathery.

4 To make noodles, roll the pasta up loosely into a roll about 7.5 cm (3 inches) wide.

5 Cut the roll into 0.5 cm (¼ inch) slices and leave for 10 minutes. Wholemeal noodles will keep for 2–3 days if covered and stored in the refrigerator.

6 To serve, cook in boiling salted water for about 8 minutes until just tender.

7 To make lasagne, cut the pasta dough into the desired size of rectangles. Leave on a floured tea towel for 10 minutes before using.

WHOLEMEAL PIZZA DOUGH

45 ml (3 tbsp) tepid milk
20 g (¾ oz) fresh yeast or 12.5 ml (2½ tsp) dried
3.75 ml (¾ tsp) raw cane sugar
300 g (11 oz) strong wholemeal flour
7.5 ml (1½ tsp) salt
30 ml (2 tbsp) olive oil
about 90 ml (6 tbsp) tepid water

1 Put the milk in a warmed jug and crumble in the fresh yeast with your fingers. If using dried yeast, sprinkle into the milk and leave in a warm place for 15 minutes until frothy. Add the sugar to the liquid and stir to dissolve, then stir in 60 ml (4 tbsp) of the flour.

2 Cover the jug with a clean tea-towel and leave in a warm place for about 30 minutes or until frothy.

3 Sift the remaining flour and the salt into a warmed large bowl. Mix in the yeast with a fork, than add the oil and enough water to draw the mixture together.

4 Turn the dough out on to a floured surface and knead for 10 minutes until it is smooth and elastic.

5 Put the ball of dough in a large floured bowl, cover with a clean tea-towel and leave in a warm place for 1½–2 hours until doubled in bulk. Use as required.

PANCAKE BATTER

MAKES 8 PANCAKES

100 g (4 oz) plain wholemeal flour
pinch of salt
1 egg
300 ml (½ pint) milk
polyunsaturated oil, for frying

1 Put the flour and salt into a bowl and make a well in the centre. Break in the egg and beat well with a wooden spoon. Gradually beat in the milk, drawing in the flour from the sides to make a smooth batter.

2 Heat a little oil in an 18 cm (7 inch) heavy-based frying pan, running it around the base and sides of the pan, until hot. Pour off any surplus.

3 Pour in just enough batter to thinly coat the base of the pan. Cook for 1–2 minutes, until golden, turn or toss and cook the second side until golden.

4 Transfer the pancake to a plate. Repeat with the remaining batter to make eight pancakes. Pile the pancakes on top of each other with greaseproof paper between each. Use as required.

NOTE

Pancake batter may also be made in a blender or food processor. Put the liquid in first, egg next and the flour last.

VARIATION

Add the grated rind of ½ a lemon or orange to the flour before mixing.

FRITTER BATTER

MAKES ABOUR 150 ML (¼ PINT)

75 g (3 oz) plain wholemeal flour
pinch of salt
15 ml (1 tbsp) polyunsaturated oil
1 egg white

1 Mix the flour and salt together in a bowl. Make a well in the centre and gradually mix in 90 ml (6 tbsp) water and the oil. Beat well until smooth.

2 Just before using the batter, whisk the egg white until stiff and fold into the batter.

VEGETABLE STOCK

MAKES ABOUT 1.2 LITRES (2 PINTS)

30 ml (2 tbsp) polyunsaturated oil
1 medium onion, skinned and finely chopped
1 medium carrot, washed and diced
50 g (2 oz) turnip, washed and diced
50 g (2 oz) parsnip, washed and diced
4 celery sticks, roughly chopped
vegetable trimmings such as: celery tops, cabbage leaves, Brussels sprouts leaves, mushroom peelings, tomato skins and potato peelings
onion skins (optional)
bouquet garni
6 whole black peppercorns

1 Heat the oil in a large saucepan, add the onion and fry gently for about 5 minutes until soft and lightly coloured. Add the vegetables to the pan with any vegetable trimmings, outer leaves or peelings available. If a dark brown coloured stock is required, add onion skins.

2 Cover the vegetables with 1.7 litres (3 pints) cold water and add the bouquet garni and peppercorns. Bring to the boil. Half cover and simmer for 1½ hours, skimming occasionally with a slotted spoon.

3 Strain the stock into a bowl and leave to cool. Cover and chill. This stock will only keep for 1–2 days.

BÉCHAMEL SAUCE

MAKES 300 ML (½ PINT)

300 ml (½ pint) milk
1 shallot, skinned and sliced, or a small piece of onion, skinned
1 small carrot, peeled and sliced
½ celery stick, chopped
1 bay leaf
3 black peppercorns
25 g (1 oz) butter or polyunsaturated margarine
25 g (1 oz) plain white or wholemeal flour
salt and pepper
30 ml (2 tbsp) single cream (optional)

1 Put the milk, vegetables and flavourings in a saucepan and slowly bring to the boil. Remove from the heat, cover and set aside to infuse for 30 minutes, then strain, reserving the milk liquid.

2 Melt the butter or margarine in a saucepan. Stir in the flour and cook gently for 1 minute, stirring. Remove the pan from the heat and gradually stir in the flavoured milk.

3 Bring to the boil and continue to cook, stirring, until the sauce thickens. Simmer very gently for 3 minutes. Remove from the heat and season with salt and pepper to taste. Stir in the cream, if using.

VARIATION

MORNAY SAUCE

Before seasoning, stir in 50 g (2 oz) finely grated, mature Cheddar cheese or 25 g (1 oz) grated Parmesan or 50 g (2 oz) grated Gruyère. Do not reheat or the cheese will become overcooked and stringy.

WHITE SAUCE

MAKES 300 ML (½ PINT)

15 g (½ oz) butter or polyunsaturated margarine
15 g (½ oz) plain white or wholemeal flour
300 ml (½ pint) milk
salt and pepper

POURING SAUCE

1 Melt the butter or margarine in a saucepan, stir in the flour and cook gently for 1 minute, stirring.

2 Remove the pan from the heat and gradually stir in the milk. Bring to the boil slowly and continue cooking, stirring all the time, until the sauce comes to the boil and thickens.

3 Simmer very gently for a further 2–3 minutes. Season with salt and pepper to taste.

COATING SAUCE

Follow the recipe for Pouring Sauce (see above), increasing butter or margarine and flour to 25 g (1 oz) each.

BINDING SAUCE

Follow the recipe for Pouring Sauce (see above), increasing butter or margarine and flour to 50 g (2 oz) each.

ONE-STAGE METHOD

1 Use ingredients in same quantities as for Pouring or Coating Sauce (see above).

2 Place the butter or margarine, flour, milk and salt and pepper to taste in a saucepan. Heat, whisking continuously, until the sauce thickens and is cooked.

BLENDER OR FOOD PROCESSOR METHOD

1 Use ingredients in same quantities as for Pouring or Coating Sauce (see above).

2 Place the butter or margarine, flour, milk and salt and pepper to taste in the machine and blend until smooth.

3 Pour into a saucepan and bring to the boil, stirring, until the sauce thickens.

VARIATIONS

PARSLEY SAUCE
Follow the recipe for the Pouring Sauce or Coating Sauce (see above).
After seasoning with salt and pepper, stir in 15–30 ml (1–2 tbsp) finely chopped fresh parsley.

ONION SAUCE
Follow the recipe for the Pouring Sauce or Coating Sauce (see above).
Soften 1 large onion, skinned and finely chopped, in the butter or margarine before adding the flour.

MUSHROOM SAUCE
Follow the recipe for the Pouring Sauce or Coating Sauce (see above).
Fry 50–75 g (2–3 oz) sliced button mushrooms in the butter or margarine before adding the flour.

CAPER SAUCE
Follow the recipe for the Pouring Sauce or Coating Sauce (see above), using all milk or – to give a better flavour – half milk and half stock.
Before seasoning with salt and pepper, stir in 15 ml (1 tbsp) capers and 5–10 ml (1–2 tsp) vinegar from the capers, or lemon juice. Reheat gently before serving.

EGG SAUCE
Follow the recipe for the Pouring Sauce or Coating Sauce (see above).
Before seasoning with salt and pepper, add 1 hard-boiled egg, shelled and chopped, and 5–10 ml (1–2 tsp) snipped chives. Reheat gently before serving.

CHEESE SAUCE
Follow the recipe for the Pouring Sauce or Coating Sauce (see above).
Before seasoning with salt and pepper, stir in 50 g (2 oz) finely grated Cheddar cheese, 2.5–5 ml (½–1 tsp) prepared mustard and a pinch of cayenne pepper.

TOMATO SAUCE

MAKES ABOUT 300 ML (½ PINT)

1 small onion, skinned and chopped
1 small carrot, peeled and chopped
25 g (1 oz) butter or margarine
25 ml (1½ tbsp) wholemeal flour
450 g (1 lb) tomatoes, quartered, or a 397 g (14 oz) can tomatoes, drained
300 ml (½ pint) vegetable stock
1 bay leaf
1 clove
2.5 ml (½ tsp) raw cane sugar
10 ml (2 tsp) tomato purée
15–60 ml (1–4 tbsp) dry white wine (optional)
salt and pepper

1 Lightly fry the onion and carrot in the butter or margarine for 5 minutes. Stir in the flour and add the tomatoes, stock, bay leaf, clove, sugar, tomato purée, wine, if used, and salt and pepper to taste.

2 Bring to the boil, cover and simmer for 30–45 minutes, or until the vegetables are cooked. Sieve, reheat and adjust seasoning, if necessary.

QUICK TOMATO SAUCE

MAKES ABOUT 450 ML (¾ PINT)

397 g (14 oz) can tomatoes
5 ml (1 tsp) tomato purée
1 small onion, skinned and chopped
1 garlic clove, skinned and crushed (optional)
pinch of dried basil
pinch of raw cane sugar
pepper
15 ml (1 tbsp) polyunsaturated oil

1 Put all the ingredients in a blender or food processor and blend until smooth.

2 Heat in a saucepan for 10–15 minutes until slightly thickened.

HOLLANDAISE SAUCE

MAKES ABOUT 300 ML (½ PINT)

30 ml (2 tbsp) wine or tarragon vinegar
2 egg yolks
225 g (8 oz) unsalted butter, softened
salt and pepper

1 Put the vinegar and 15 ml (1 tbsp) water into a saucepan. Boil gently until the liquid has reduced by half. Set aside until cool.

2 Put the egg yolks and reduced vinegar liquid into a double saucepan or bowl standing over a pan of very gently simmering water. Whisk until the mixture is thick and fluffy.

3 Gradually add the butter, a tiny piece at a time. Whisk briskly until each piece has been absorbed by the sauce and the sauce itself is the consistency of mayonnaise. Season with salt and pepper. If the sauce is too sharp, add a little more butter – it should be slightly piquant and warm, rather than hot, when served.

VARIATION

MOUSSELINE SAUCE

This is a richer sauce suitable for asparagus and broccoli. Stir 45 ml (3 tbsp) whipped double cream into the sauce just before serving.

COCONUT MILK

MAKES 450 ML (¾ PINT) THICK COCONUT MILK OR 600 ML (1 PINT) THIN COCONUT MILK

198 g (7 oz) packet creamed coconut

1 Break the coconut into a bowl. Add 450 ml (¾ pint) warm water. Stir until dissolved. This will make a thick milk. Strain through muslin or a fine sieve before use.

2 For a thinner milk, stir in an extra 150 ml (¼ pint) water. Strain through muslin or a fine sieve before use.

SAVOURY CRUMBLE

175 g (6 oz) plain wholemeal flour
75 g (3 oz) butter or polyunsaturated margarine
5 ml (1 tsp) chopped fresh herbs or 2.5 ml (½ tsp) dried mixed herbs
salt and pepper

1 Put the flour in a bowl and rub in the butter or margarine until the mixture resembles fine crumbs. Stir in the herbs and salt and pepper to taste.

2 Sprinkle the mixture on top of a casserole or gratin dish and bake in the oven at 200°C (400°F) mark 6 for about 30 minutes until golden.

SWEDE AND POTATO LATTICE

350 g (12 oz) potato, peeled
350 g (12 oz) swede, peeled
salt and pepper
25 g (1 oz) butter or polyunsaturated margarine
25 g (1 oz) Cheddar cheese, grated

1 Cook the potato and swede in boiling salted water until tender. Drain very well, then push through a mouli or wire sieve.

2 Beat in the butter or margarine, then season with salt and pepper to taste. Pipe or spoon over a casserole, sprinkle the cheese on top and flash under the grill to brown.

BOILED RICE

SERVES 4

225 g (8 oz) long grain brown rice
salt

Method One

1 Put 3.4 litres (6 pints) water in a large saucepan and bring to a fast boil. Add the rice and salt to taste.

2 Stir once to loosen the grains at the base of the pan, then leave, uncovered, to cook for 35 minutes until tender.

3 Drain well, rinse with hot water and drain again. Pour into a warmed serving dish and separate the grains with a fork.

Method Two

Allow 600 ml (1 pint) water to 225 g (8 oz) long grain brown rice. Put the rice, salt to taste and water in a saucepan and bring quickly to the boil, stir well and cover with a tightly fitting lid. Reduce the heat and simmer for 35 minutes until tender and the water has been absorbed. Separate the grains with a fork before serving.

VARIATIONS

Although rice is most usually cooked in water, it can also be cooked in other liquids to give extra flavour and variety. The water may be replaced by vegetable stock or canned tomato juice, undiluted or used half and half with water.

HERBY RICE
Add a pinch of dried herbs with the cooking liquid (eg sage, marjoram, thyme, mixed herbs).

SAFFRON RICE
Add a pinch of ground saffron to the cooking water to give the rice a delicate yellow colour.

Soak a good pinch of saffron strands in a little boiling water for 15 minutes, then add to the rice before cooking.

TURMERIC RICE
Also used to give rice a yellow colour, but add only a pinch of turmeric to the cooking water as it has a more pronounced colour.

BROWN RICE RISOTTO

SERVES 4

45 ml (3 tbsp) polyunsaturated oil
2 medium onions, skinned and sliced
225 g (8 oz) long grain brown rice
5 ml (1 tsp) turmeric
600 ml (1 pint) vegetable stock
salt and pepper
chopped fresh parsley, to garnish

1 Heat the oil in a medium flameproof casserole, add the onions, rice and turmeric and fry gently for 1–2 minutes. Stir in the stock and salt and pepper to taste. Bring to the boil.

2 Cover the dish tightly and cook at 170°C (325°F) mark 3 for about 1 hour, until the rice is tender and the stock absorbed. Adjust the seasoning and garnish with plenty of chopped parsley.

GARLIC BREAD

SERVES 8–10

1 large wholemeal French-style loaf
100–175 g (4–6 oz) butter or polyunsaturated margarine
2 garlic cloves, skinned and crushed
salt and pepper

1 Cut the loaf into 2.5 cm (1 inch) thick slices.

2 Cream the butter or margarine in a bowl until soft. Add the garlic and salt and pepper to taste and beat together.

3 Spread liberally between the slices. Wrap the loaf loosely in foil and bake at 180°C (350°F) mark 4 for about 15 minutes until soft.

VARIATION

HERB BREAD
Follow the recipe above, omitting the garlic and adding 30 ml (2 tbsp) fresh chopped herbs, eg parsley, chives, thyme.

NATURAL YOGURT

MAKES 600 ML (1 PINT)

568 ml (1 pint) pasteurised or UHT milk
15 ml (1 tbsp) natural yogurt
15 ml (1 tbsp) skimmed milk powder (optional)

1 Sterilise all your containers and utensils with boiling water or a recommended sterilising solution. Warm a wide-necked insulated jar.

2 Pour the milk into a saucepan and bring to the boil. Remove from the heat and leave the milk to cool to 43°C (110°F) on a thermometer, or blood temperature. If using UHT milk, there is no need to boil: just heat to the correct temperature.

3 Spoon the yogurt into a bowl and stir in a little of the cooled milk. Add the milk powder, if used, to make a paste. (This helps make a thick yogurt.)

4 Stir in the remaining milk and pour the mixture into the warmed insulated jar. Replace the lid and leave for 6–8 hours, undisturbed, until set. Do not move the jar or the yogurt will not set.

5 As soon as the yogurt has set, transfer to the refrigerator to chill. When cold, use as required. Yogurt can be stored for up to 5 days in the refrigerator.

CROÛTONS

SERVES 4

2 slices of wholemeal bread
polyunsaturated oil, for frying

1 Trim the crusts off the bread slices and cut them into 0.5–1 cm (¼–½ inch) cubes.

2 Heat at least 0.5 cm (¼ inch) of oil in a heavy-based frying pan and fry the bread cubes until crisp and golden. Keep stirring the croûtons while they are frying.

3 Lift the croûtons out of the pan all at once and drain on absorbent kitchen paper.
Croûtons should be passed around in a separate bowl to be added to each bowl of soup at the last moment; otherwise they may go soggy.

MELBA TOAST

SERVES 4

4 slices of thick cut ready-sliced brown bread

1 Preheat the grill and toast the bread on both sides until golden brown.

2 Using a serrated knife, cut off the crusts and slide the knife between the toasted edges to split the bread.

3 Cut each piece in half diagonally. Place on a baking sheet and bake at 150°C (300°F) mark 2 for 15–20 minutes until curled dry and brittle.

4 Serve while still warm. If it is made ahead, store it in an airtight container, then refresh it for a short time in the oven.

INDEX